HOW THE F**K DID I LOSE MY TIARA?

A True Story of Survival, Self-Worth, and Starting Over.

Written By Lisa Holley Palmer

Title: *How The F**K Did I Lose My Tiara?*

Author: Lisa Holley Palmer

This is a true account based on the author's personal experiences. For privacy and legal reasons, names, identifying details, and some circumstances have been changed or omitted. The author has made every effort to portray events accurately and truthfully to the best of hermemory and interpretation.

This book is a work of nonfiction. The views and opinions expressed are solely those of theauthor.

Editor Acknowledgment Editor
Jennifer Charlinski

Finding the right editor for a deeply personal book is no easy task. I wasn't just looking for someone with technical skills; I wanted someone intuitive, intelligent, articulate, and most importantly, honest. I didn't want a "yes person"; I needed someone who would tell it to me straight, challenge me when necessary, and truly understand the heart of what I was writing.

When Jenn and I first connected via email, something just clicked. We followed up with a Zoom call, and while Jenn didn't give much away initially, it was clear she was listening—really listening. Her calm, focused presence and quiet intellect stood out immediately. She absorbed everything I said without jumping in, and that told me I'd foundsomeone who takes her craft seriously.

I was also hoping to work with someone who was spiritually attuned—someone who couldunderstand the deeper layers of my story beyond just grammar and structure. Jenn ticked every box.

I'm confident we have a bestseller in the making, and I know I couldn't have done it withoutJenn's guidance, wisdom, and sharp editorial insight. Thank you, Jenn, for your professionalism, your presence, and your rare ability to truly hear the voice of a writer.

For my son, my one true love.

I am so deeply blessed to have you in my life.

Through the hardest moments, your little smile or cheeky banter carried me through morethan you'll ever know.

There were times I wasn't sure I could keep going, but you gave me purpose, strength, andthe will to rise again.

Without you, I can honestly say I would not be here.

You are my light in the darkest room, my reason, my miracle.

And when I'm no longer around to remind you of your strength,I leave you this poem—a seed to carry in your heart.

When the Time Comes (*For my son*)

Sometimes, you have to grow in the dark.No sun, no map, just a quiet spark.

The world feels heavy, cold, and wide— But trust me, love, there's strength inside.

It might get hard, it might feel slow, Like nothing's changing, nothing grows.But deep in silence, roots take hold,

And broken soil makes brave hearts bold.

You won't always see the reason why— Some days you'll hurt, some days you'll cry.But pain can shape the softest soul,

And cracks can make the broken whole.

Table of Contents

CHAPTER ONE:

In the Shadows of Loss

September 13

The room was silent except for the sound of my shallow breathing. My fingers tightened around my phone, the screen lighting up with yet another notification. Ping. My stomach twisted, and a familiar ache clawed at my chest as my heart pounded against my ribs. How much more could I take?

I wasn't a hostage. But I felt like one.

The window was locked—I'd checked it twice. The door? Double-checked. Locked. My phone was my lifeline, my only connection to safety if I had to call the police again. But even that felt fragile, like it might shatter in my grip.

I was over 40 years of age, yet there I was—cowering in my parents' spare room like a frightened child. Sleep came in restless, fractured moments. But waking was worse.

Waking meant facing reality.

The messages had started again. The relentless, abusive texts. The calls—one after another. I never answered, but he never stopped. It was Groundhog Day, only darker.

He was back. The angry bear had returned.

The snake spewing venom and spitting threats. Death threats. 83 missed calls. 28 messages. And it wasn't even 8 a.m.

7:33 a.m. Missed call.

Ping. **Answer your phone.** Ping. **I won't go away**

Ping. Lisa, you've woken the angry bear

Four missed calls. Ping. **You have nothing left** Fourteen missed calls. Ping. **Fat girls are all the same**Eleven missed calls. Ping. **Fat. That's what you are** Eighteen missed calls. Ping. **Wrong**

Ping. I didn't say that. You're hearing things again

Five missed calls. Ping. **I'm coming round**

Three missed calls. Ping. Seven missed calls. Ping. Seven more. Ping.

Eight. Ping.

Six. Ping. **WELL DONE. Now I'm going to kill you**

And then—the emails. Ominous. Chilling. Each word a quiet threat.

I hadn't spoken to him in weeks. I hadn't responded at all. But it didn't matter. Hewouldn't STOP.

For the second time in a week, he'd turned up. My mum and I, frozen in fear, scrambling to call the police. Doors locked. Windows shut. Lights off.

Trapped. Again.

I thought this relationship would be different.

I had already escaped one abusive relationship. Survived one nightmare.

How could I have been so wrong?

How much more? How much more pain, more fear, more running?

I was homeless. Again. The first time, I had nowhere to go. This time, losing everything I'd built. Middle-aged and with no choice but to go back to my parents' house—because I had nowhere else.

It was exhausting—mentally and physically. But this time was worse. This time, the fear had been clinging to me like a second skin, tightening with every breath.

How could I have ended up in the same situation, yet somehow even more terrified?

You see, I had already left a marriage once before and escaped with just my son, the clothes on my back, and £250 to my name. We ended up in a damp, mould-ridden mobile caravan with no toilet. Just a bucket outside.

I swore I would never go back to that kind of life. I swore I would never let it happen again.

And yet . . . there I was.

The darkness had crept back in, curling around my mind, whispering in my ear.

There's only one way out.

Fear does this—it traps you and tricks you into silence. It makes you doubt yourself, makes you wonder if maybe . . . just maybe, you deserve it.

I'd heard his voice twisting in the dark, venom dripping from every word. I felt his weight, crushing the air from my lungs, pressing me down until I was nothing. I saw his eyes—empty, lifeless—as if the man I thought I knew had been swallowed whole bysomething monstrous.

And there I sat. Shaking. Hiding. Wondering how it came to this.

The messages had been relentless. The vile texts, the calls, the threats—each one gnawing away at me, more than the last, like rust on steel.

"Why? Why was this happening to me, God?"I've only ever tried to help.

***

Sleep had been a distant dream.

My body felt drained—mentally, physically, emotionally. Every muscle ached, heavywith exhaustion, yet sleep never came. My mind wouldn't let it. Every time I closed my eyes, I was back there—trapped beneath him, gasping for air, clawing for escape.

Even while safe in my parents' house, my chest felt tight, like phantom pressure stillhad me pinned down. Was I even safe? The walls felt too thin, the locks too fragile. Every shadow stretched too far. Every creak in the floorboards made my pulse spike, and my breathhitch.

I ran my fingers over my wrist, tracing the faint bruises left behind—ugly remindersthat my body remembered what I wanted to forget. The panic lived inside me now, coiled tight, waiting to strike.

And the exhaustion? It wasn't just in my bones—it was in my soul. I wasn't just tired. I was worn down. Hollowed out. A version of myself I barely recognised.

My mum and I sat side by side—hiding. She was scared.

It was ludicrous—two grown women, cowering in fear. But have you ever seen someone so enraged, so consumed by darkness, that they've become unrecognisable? I had. And it left me shattered.

I glanced at my mum, her hands clasped tightly in her lap, knuckles white. The house felt too small, too fragile to protect us. She wasn't just afraid—she was helpless. The protective mother in her wanted to shield me, but outside that door, the threat was too great, and the fear too real.

We could hear his voice from outside, low and menacing, twisted by rage. I could feel the air vibrating with his anger. My mum's eyes were fixed on the door, as if somehow, she might will him to go away. Her lips trembled, but she said nothing. There was nothing left to say. She had watched me escape once before, seen me rebuild my life from nothing, and now, there we were again, on the edge of terror.

I could feel her fighting against the same wave of panic that was threatening to consume me. She wasn't just trying to keep herself calm; she was trying to keep me calm, too. But how do you reassure someone when you're both terrified of what's on the other side of the door? She couldn't fix it. This time, all she could do was sit beside me, both of us trembling, as we waited for the storm to pass.

As usual, while lying in bed later that night, dreadful memories flashed back. One night, in particular, resurfaced with chilling clarity, as if it had happened just yesterday.

I had gone to bed around 10 p.m. and my dog Holly, curled up beside me—with gentle warmth yet small comfort. Damien was passed out on the sofa, snoring heavily. When he was comatose, you never woke him. It wasn't safe.

Somewhere after midnight, I jolted awake in sheer terror. His knee was pressed into my chest, crushing me. I couldn't breathe. My mind scrambled to catch up with the panic flooding my body as I gasped for air, eyes wide, struggling. His voice, thick and slurred, filled the darkness.

"Give it to me."

My heart pounded. Wh—what? Give you what? "Your phone."

I gestured weakly towards the bedside table. It's right there . . . take it. I've got nothing to hide.

He snatched it and stumbled out of the room, leaving me shaking, tears rolling silently down my face. My body trembled uncontrollably. What had just happened? Why? Fear wrapped its icy grip around me so tightly that I felt paralysed. For the rest of the night, I lay in silence, too afraid to move, too afraid to cry out.

But I should have known. At the start, it didn't seem like a problem. Damien would have a few drinks at night or a couple on weekends, just like anyone else—a cider while watching the game, a glass of wine with dinner. It felt normal, even social. He'd laugh it off if I ever mentioned it. "It's just to unwind," he'd say, his tone light, convincing. And I believed him. Why wouldn't I? It wasn't like he was stumbling around or slurring his words. He was charming and in control.

14

Looking back, he would go into the bath for an hour or so—he said it was his 'time to relax.'Hindsight is a curious thing; I'm sure he'd been drinking, but I didn't realise then. Instead, I thought, *He can't be an alcoholic—he'd be flailing all over the place.*

Of course, after we moved in together things began to shift. The drinking crept into weeknights, always with an excuse—a tough day at work, a disagreement with a friend, thestress of life piling up. He'd hide it well at first, brushing off my concerns with a smile or ajoke.

But then came the nights when he'd sit in tears, clutching a can of cider, sobbingabout the children he no longer saw. "I can't cope," he'd whisper, his voice cracking.

And I, ever the rescuer—the kind of person who couldn't help but step in—needed to. Seeing someone upset or in pain twisted something inside me, and if I could ease their suffering, I would, whether I knew them well or not. What was wrong with me? Why did Ifeel this way?

I held him. Whispered promises: "We'll get through this together."

Was being kind such a crime?

I told myself it was just a phase, that he was grieving, that he needed my support. Butthat night . . . that night was different. It was worse. There was a darkness in him I had neverseen before, a shadow that seemed to seep from his very pores, distorting the air around him into something heavy, suffocating.

It had started so normally—my son out for the night, the two of us watching a film together.Cosy. Calm. But later, as I stayed up to read, I noticed Damien lingering in the next room, standing in the shadows of the office. Just . . . watching.

His eyes were different. Lifeless. Cold. Like the soul behind them had retreated into someabyss.

"Are you okay?" I asked, trying to keep my voice steady.

Something twisted in his expression, and before I could react, his hands were around mythroat.

"You liar!" he screamed. "You lying-whore!"

He was calling me her name—his ex's name. I choked, clawing at his grip, the air stolenfrom my lungs.

"I'm not her! Please . . . let go!" I begged, my voice strangled and raw.

In that excruciating moment, every fibre of my being had been consumed by terror. My vision tunnelled, and the edges of the room faded into a blur of shadows and pain. I felt his grip tightening, the pressure around my throat like an iron vice, slowly crushing my will to breathe. Every heartbeat pounded in my ears, a frantic drum of desperation; a warning thatmy time was running out.

My lungs burned for air that wouldn't come, and each laboured gasp was a futile plea against the suffocating darkness encroaching on my senses. I tried to scream, to reach out for help, but the sound that emerged was nothing more than a strangled whisper. The taste of fear was bitter on my tongue, and my thoughts spun wildly—a chaotic mix of memories and panic, desperate to find an escape from this living nightmare.

The world narrowed to the terrifying reality of his hands, the coarse pressure of his grip, and the overwhelming sense of impending doom. Cold sweat trickled down my skin and mingled with tears I couldn't hold back. Every second stretched interminably; a silent testament to the horror of being so utterly powerless.

And in that desperate, paralysing moment, as the weight of his fury and my terror bore down on me, I realised with shattering clarity that nothing in that darkness was as I had ever known it before. I was lost, clinging to a fragile hope that somehow, against all odds, I might still find a way to survive.

Suddenly, he shoved me backwards, spinning me as his fist slammed into the wall beside the mirror with a force that made the entire room shudder. The impact echoed like a gunshot, and I flinched, my heart pounding so fiercely I feared it might burst. The mirror didn't shatter outright, but it rattled violently, the glass warping as though it might break at any moment.

I stood frozen, my whole body trembling like a leaf caught in a tempest, my breath imprisoned in my throat.

For a long, agonising moment, his hand hung in the air—clenched and quivering—before he slowly turned to face me. His eyes were wild, unhinged; the look on his face was not mere anger, but something far darker, something I could not name.

Then, instinct took over. I bolted, fleeing up the stairs as my legs barely carried me, my vision blurring with tears. I slammed the bedroom door shut, fumbling with the lock until it clicked securely into place. I pressed my back against the door, my hands clamped over my mouth to stifle the sobs wracking my chest.

Yet even through the barrier of the door, I could sense him—waiting. Watching. And I knew, deep in my bones, that the lock would never be enough to keep that dreadful presence at bay. And then came the morning.

The house was suffocatingly silent. My son had stayed out, thank God. But I could feel it—like the air itself was holding its breath. My heart was a relentless drum, each beat echoing louder as I crept out of my room. Each step down the stairs felt like descendingdeeper into a nightmare.

Then I heard him.

"Tea? Want some breakfast?"

His voice was calm. Cheerful. As if nothing had happened. As if he hadn't just tried to kill me mere hours before.

I felt bile rise in my throat. How dare he?

I confronted him. "Do you even remember what you did last night? I vowed no man wouldever lay a hand on me again. You— what you did was unforgivable."

But *how* was this happening again?I had been here before.

There'd been a different man—John. A different nightmare. But the same fear. In the end, I had nothing. No home, no money, no plan—just the desperate need to escape. I sat in the car, my hands gripping the steering wheel so tightly my knuckles ached. The rain pounded against the windscreen, drowning out everything but the frantic thud of my own heart.

I glanced in the rear-view mirror at my son, curled up in the backseat. Peaceful. Unaware ofthe storm raging inside me. I had left a man once before. And here I was again.

But to understand how I ended up in the same predicament— staring at the edge of despair, clutching the last threads of my strength—you need to know where it all began.

***

I wasn't a planned pregnancy, and my arrival had felt like an intrusion rather than a celebration. I emerged into a household where grief lingered like a perpetual fog. My parents, still reeling from the loss of my grandad—a man whose laughter once filled our home—had dreams and ambitions that did not include a child. "Born at the wrong time,"they would say.

My grandad had been the heartbeat of our family, a charming, larger-than-life figure whose absence left a void. His death was not just a loss—the silence swallowed their laughter and dimmed their hope. And in that suffocating atmosphere of sorrow, I arrived: a tiny, fragile life, pressing against the heavy grip of grief.

As I grew, I learned early that love in our home was a quiet, almost invisible thing. I craved the warmth and connection I saw in other families, yet in ours, affection was scarce—a lingering echo of what once was. So, I became an observer, as a means to shrinkinto the margins, waiting for the moment to feel seen.

And then Damien entered my life. He was the promise of a second chance, the one who made me believe, if only for a little while, that I mattered. Yet even as I clung to him, a quiet voice inside wondered if I was trading one form of invisibility for another. His temper often flared unpredictably as his eyes darkened with an unnamed menace. I began to fear that I was repeating the patterns of my past.

Even as I sat there with Mum, shaking behind a locked fucking door, one thought wouldn't leave me: Did I do this? Had this been all Damien—or had I let this happen? It felt like the terror had my name written on it. Like I'd somehow earned it.

Maybe if I hadn't ignored my gut. Maybe if I'd walked away the first time. Maybe if I wasn't so desperate to feel loved, or worthy, or anything at all—maybe then I wouldn't be here, hiding, broken, afraid.

I hated myself for not seeing it sooner. For letting it get this far. For still questioning whether it was me that brought the monster to the door. The thought was as relentless as it was chilling.

In trying to understand the roots of my unworthiness, I began to unravel the tapestry of my family's past. My dad's story, in particular, is a thread woven with hardship and silent determination.

He grew up knowing scarcity—an emptiness that seemed to etch itself into his very bones. I can still hear his steady yet strained voice as he recalled the day he witnessed his father collapse under the crushing weight of debt. The sight of his father's tears, so rare on a man's face, left an indelible scar on him. And then there was his mother—distant and elusive—a presence that hovered like a ghost in his childhood memories, there yet absent in every tangible way. That void, that absence of true nurture, shaped his view of women into one of guarded mistrust, even resentment. To him, love had always been tangled with pain—a fragile trust he could never fully extend.

Witnessing his father unravel under financial strain forged a relentless determination in my dad. He swore that he would never be caught in that same suffocating grip. Money became both his shield and his weapon—a means to fortify himself against any vulnerability. Success, wealth, and security took centre stage, pushing feelings, family, and even tenderness to the margins. His mission was clear: to build an empire, to prove that he was enough—no matter the cost.

And then, there was my mum. In contrast to my dad's

careful, deliberate way of navigating the world—his kindness often tucked beneath a reserved exterior, my mum was like a burst of sunlight—carefree, her heart too big for her own good, always eager to smooth rough edges and keep the peace. I share their stories because I want you to understand how our parents' journeys, with all their triumphs and heartaches, shape us in ways we might not immediately realise. By the end of this book, you'll see how their stories wove into mine, leaving marks that are both invisible and indelible.

***

Before meeting my dad, my mum had loved another deeply. There was another man in her past—a man whose heart was as expansive as the horizon, offering her a chance at a life across the Atlantic. He had been offered his dream job in Canada and pleaded with her to join him. But family ties, the unyielding bonds of responsibility and tradition, held her back. Not long after that bittersweet choice, fate intervened at a party where she met my dad.

Perhaps she even hoped that my arrival might one day soften the weight of her past sorrows. But grief, as I learned all too well, is relentless—it does not fade with new beginnings.

She kept the house warm, ensured meals were always ready, and gave herself fully to her role as a devoted wife. Yet, in their marriage, love wasn't marked by grand gestures or shared smiles; it was a quiet, steadfast connection—a partnership built on mutual respect and shared purpose. I never witnessed them holding hands or exchanging affectionate words.

Love, as it was expressed in our home, was something unspoken—a quiet assurance rather than something openly celebrated.

I have no memory of my dad's arms enveloping me in a comforting embrace, nor of his gentle goodnight kisses. There was one moment—a painfully awkward, heartbreaking attempt at a hug—when he brusquely said, "Get off," as if he couldn't bear the vulnerability. It wasn't that he didn't care; he simply didn't know how to offer love. To him, love was a matter of survival—a hard, unyielding shield against a world that had taught him only to fend for himself.

Now, as an adult piecing together the fragments of my past, I see the layers of pain behind that rejection. But as a child, I was left questioning: What's wrong with me? Am I unlovable? In those formative years—those early, impressionable years up to the age of seven—the feeling of being unwanted settled in and began to shape who I would become.

This isn't a hard-luck story, nor is it a tale of despair. It's a journey of coming to understand that every moment of tragedy and every unspoken grief was, in some mysterious way, meant to teach me something. My dad's unresolved wounds, and his fractured relationship with his mother, rendered him incapable of expressing love in the way I needed.

To soothe my nan's lingering grief, my parents inadvertently made her the centre of our world—my sanctuary and haven. They hadn't intended to leave me feeling abandoned, but as a small child, it often felt as though I was less of a priority, less wanted. The bond I longed to share with them never fully formed, leaving a quiet, persistent gap in every interaction.

Yet, my nan was my sanctuary. She had an endless capacity for warmth and kindness.

I spent countless hours in her sunlit garden, where the earthy scent of damp soil and blooming flowers would wrap around us like a healing balm. With her, I felt safe—content among my teddies and the gentle love that only she could provide.

I was always searching for that missing piece—the kind of love I saw freely given in other families. So, when Damien entered my life, it felt as though fate had finally brought me what I'd been yearning for. I didn't know then that fate, with its dark sense of humour, had a way of twisting hope into something altogether different.

CHAPTER TWO:

Tagged as a Dunce

A Misfit's Story

Then school started. I can't say I remember much of primary school, but starting secondary was a whole different beast. I walked into that new, massive school with a cocktail of excitement and sheer terror. The older kids loomed like giants, and the whole place felt like a maze where I was doomed to get lost. And then came the legendary horror stories: "If they don't like you, they'll shove your head down the toilet and flush it!" Seriously—just what a kid needs to hear on their first day. It wasn't true, of course, but that fear stuckaround.

The night before, I was a total wreck. My nerves were on high alert, excitement battling anxiety until, unsurprisingly, anxiety won. My parents didn't have much money backthen—and even when they did, they were tighter than a jar lid. Proper tight sods, really.

Then there was PE. I still remember those dodgy, lightweight plimsoll shoes from Woolworths—the ones that practically screamed, "I cost £2 and smell like regret!" That was all I had. They reeked of cheap rubber, not the fresh, new-shoe smell that everyone else seemed to enjoy. I was convinced I was the only kid in school rocking them, like a walkingclearance rack.

Some kids were catalogue kids—you know, the ones with trainers, tracksuits, and the whole kit from the Freemans or Littlewoods, bought on credit. It was brilliant for them; they had everything, and their parents just paid it off in instalments. And me? I wasn't even in the running. I was one grade below the catalogue kid standard because my parents, those miserly sods, wouldn't pay the interest! I mean, come on—it wasn't like it was a mortgage. Instead, I had to make do with my Woolies' plimsolls, feeling like a budget superhero in a world of stylish clones. very time I saw someone sporting Reebok Classics or those flashy red Nike trainers, I was proper fuming. Pissed off doesn't even begin to cover it—a young teenager desperate to make an impression, feeling invisible amongst a sea of catalogue kids.

But as embarrassing as it all felt that misfit feeling became a part of me. I learned to laugh at it, to own it. Because, in the end, being a misfit meant I saw the world a bit differently—less black and white—and that made all the difference.

Then there were the school dinners. Funny how some memories stick, isn't it? I still remember the way lunchtime felt like a mix of excitement and dread. If you had a nice lunchbox, you became an instant target—some kids wouldn't just share, they'd outright nick your food. My mum, ever so loving, packed me the same humble meal nearly every day: a sandwich (usually ham, always dry), a piece of fruit—more often than not a rock-hard apple—and the pièce de resistance—a Club biscuit. That Club biscuit was the highlight of my day—a little slice of joy amidst a sea of mediocrity. Of course, there were those greedy sods who thought it was fair game to steal it. Regularly, it would vanish before I even got to savour it.

Then there were the other, more mischievous moments of

school life—like snoggingbehind the bike sheds. I remember my first proper boyfriend; I really liked him. We'd time our snogs like it was some sort of Olympic event. "47 seconds this time— new personal best!" We must've looked absolutely daft, but at that age, it felt like the pinnacle of rebellionand excitement.

Yet, as the years went on, a heavier shadow began to settle over my school days. I felt different. While my classmates seemed to breeze through reading and writing, I struggledto make sense of words on a page. When I opened a book, it was like staring out at a vast, churning sea—letters and words would swim and blur together as if they were having a party that I wasn't invited to. Grammar rules—like when to use 'there' versus 'their'—were mysteries written in an indecipherable code. I just couldn't keep up, and it wasn't long before everyone noticed. I became labelled as the "dunce." A name slapped on as if that defined my entire worth.

I was in school during the 80s, and if you were seen as struggling, you were quicklyconsigned to the bottom sets. I still recall the terror of being forced to stand in front of the class to read aloud. I'd stammer through my words, "I . . . I . . . h–h–have . . ." while the other kids sniggered behind me. They didn't understand. To them, I was just slow and stupid and they made sure everyone knew it.

Being placed in those lower sets came with its stigma: stupid. Dumb. Not good enough. I could see it in the way teachers looked at me—part pity, part disappointment, and sometimes even outright indifference. Strangely, at first, I didn't mind too much. Some of the fun boys were in those groups too, and I realised they weren't inherently stupid—they just learned differently, like me. School was always more about regurgitating facts than truly understanding them. Who cared when King

George died? My brain simply wouldn't hold onto it, no matter how hard I tried. And then came the real humiliation—the special bus. I can still hear the cruel whispers and mocking laughter. The teasing was relentless. I remember the snide remarks that cut deep: "How many windows are you gonna lick today?" they'd sneer, their voicesdripping with mockery. At first, I tried to shield myself with humour—if they called me thick, I'd laugh and reply, "Only two windows today!" But behind the smiles, I was drowning in shame and that's when the dread began.

I remember standing in the queue for the special bus, my feet frozen to the groundlike they were made of stone. I refused to get on. My stomach twisted itself into knots as I glanced around, pretending not to see the stares—but I felt them. Every single one. The names, the looks, the sniggers—they're etched into my memory like cruel graffiti I can't scrub clean. "Doh." "Div." "Spaz."

They weren't just childish insults—they were confirmations of everything I feared was true. That I was stupid. That I was slow. That I didn't belong.

I didn't even really understand what dyslexia was back then—no one explained it to me. All I knew was that the words wouldn't stay still, that I couldn't read properly, that the page would blur or twist or simply refuse to make sense. And because of that, I became a target.

Every mistake I made felt like public proof that I wasn't good enough. That I was broken in some way no one could—or would—fix. My cheeks burned constantly, not just from shame, but from the ache of trying to hold it together. I started to dread school—notbecause of the lessons, but because of the weight of being *seen*. Saw, for what I feared I really was: a failure.

Inside, I began to shrink. I laughed along with the jokes made at my expense, just to keep the peace, just to survive. But inside, I was crumbling. I hated being there. I hated myself for not being able to keep up. I hated the part of me that wanted so badly to be accepted, even while knowing I wasn't.

The shame wasn't just about reading or spelling—it became a part of my identity. I started to believe that I was the problem. That no matter how hard I tried, I'd never measure up. The confidence I might have had when I first walked into school— whatever tiny spark of it there was—got snuffed out early. And once it was gone, I didn't know how to get it back.

I stopped raising my hand. I stopped trying. What was the point? I began to bunk off whenever I could, convincing myself I didn't care. But the truth? I cared so much it hurt. I just didn't know how to keep caring and keep surviving at the same time. So, I disappeared into the background. And when that wasn't enough, I became the joker. If they were going to laugh, at least I'd control the punchline.

But behind the smile, behind the act, was a girl who felt worthless. A girl who couldn't understand why she couldn't just be like everyone else. A girl who was already learning to wear masks to hide the parts of herself she thought no one could ever love.

It wasn't an easy existence, feeling so different and so isolated. But looking back now,

I realise that every painful moment, every sneer and every cruel joke, helped shape me into someone who eventually learned to see the world from a different perspective—a perspective that, while born of pain, also became a source of strength and empathy. And in that strange, perverse way, being the misfit shaped me into the person I was meant to be.

***

Bunking off became a regular thing. It was either me and one of my best pals, or sometimesjust me. I laugh now because you'd think Tommy was one of the cool kids—he had that London vibe. I remember when his family moved up from London; they were proper cool.

His dad was a total legend—absolutely mad, but in the best way. I just loved being around him. One winter, it was snowing, and he tied us to the back of his truck with ropes and droveus up the hill so we could sledge down. Bloody brilliant, he was.

And his brother? Oh, his brother is now a very famous DJ, but back then, he was justthe lad we laughed with. Still, me and his brother got on so well. Tommy and I had our little routine sorted: get on the bus in the morning, let everyone else jump off for school, and we'dstay hidden at the back. Then we'd sneak off a few stops later like we were masterminds of bunking.

After that, we'd go on our so-called 'survival trips.' Honestly, just thinking about it now makes me laugh. He'd hold up a loaf of bread like some kind of proud hunter-gatherer, grinning, "Lis, sorted the food!" Like we were about to have a three-course meal in the wilderness. Meanwhile, I'd casually pull out a pack of ten Silk Cut cigs, shrug, and say, "Didn't have enough for a drink."

He'd stare at me, shaking his head in mock despair. "How the hell are we supposed tosurvive on that?"

God knows what Bear Grylls, the infamous adventurer and survivalist, would have said. Probably something about drinking our own wee and foraging for insects. But that was the thing—we thought we were thriving. We weren't just bunking off school; we were living.

We'd disappear into the park or the woods for hours—five, six, sometimes even seven—talking absolute rubbish, daring each other to do stupid things, or just lying on the grass, watching the clouds drift by. It was freedom, pure and simple. And to us, that loaf of bread and those cigarettes? That was survival.

And then there was my other friend, Sian. She hated school just as much as I did, so we had our little escape plan. Lunchtime would roll around, and instead of heading to the canteen, we'd sneak off, hop onto the milk float with Chris the milkman, and he'd drive us back to her house like some kind of dodgy school run service. We thought we were geniuses. Absolute masterminds. Once there, we'd raid the kitchen, eat a Pot Noodle, and stretch out on the sofa, feeling like we were living the dream. No teachers, no boring lessons—just us, a daytime TV show in the background, and the sheer thrill of getting away with it.

The only problem? Have you ever tried to use a milk float as a getaway car? Don't. It tops out at about 10 or 15 mph on a good day. Even worse, Sian's mum worked in the village shop—right in the centre of the one-way system. And of course, the entire village revolved around that bloody one-way road. Cars would stop, people would reverse, and there we were—two kids practically plastered to the floor of a milk float with no doors and massive windows. If you think hiding in a milk float is easy, trust me, it's not. Every time we passed her mum's shop, we'd duck so fast it was like a dubious game of whack-a-mole, our hearts hammering in our chests.

Frankly, the mere idea brings a smile to my face now. Half my school life wasn't even about school—it'd been about escaping it, about the friends who made all the crap bits bearable.

Those stupid, reckless, brilliant moments. They were good times. The best times, even.

There was one instance that'd been particularly funny. It was summer, roasting hot, and we'd gone back to my friend's house. We got the garden hose out and started spraying each other, having a laugh. Then, for reasons only a kid could explain, we decided to start spraying cars as they went by. I know, naughty, but in my defence, I was just a kid! Anyway, we were spraying cars and giggling behind the hedge like proper little troublemakers when the next car pulled up. We hid behind the hedge, thumb over the hose, ready for the next victim.

Suddenly, we heard screeching brakes. We peeked out and—oh my days—it was an old Metro police car. And their window was open! To be fair, they weren't that wet, but they gave us a proper rollicking and marched us straight back to school. Mortifying.

But if school life wasn't humiliating enough, there was a darker, more chilling secret lurking in the shadows of my childhood.

I was at home, minding my own business when the first phone call came through; a deep, unnervingly calm voice spoke into the receiver, "Lisa, I saw you today. Walking down the high street in your long socks and school skirt." I froze. My heart hammered in my chest as I tried to convince myself it was just one of the boys playing a prank. Mustering what little courage I had, I snapped. "Stop it!" I yelled, before slamming the phone down. Yet beneath that anger, a cold terror had taken hold.

The next day at school, I couldn't concentrate. I was constantly scanning every face, every laugh, every whisper, wondering if someone was in on it. "Was it them?" I'd ask myself repeatedly. But I said nothing; I thought it would all pass. That night, there was no

call, and for a brief, fleeting moment, I allowed myself to hope that it had been a one-offincident. I tried to shrug it off.

Then, two days later, the phone rang again. This time, my mum answered. I listened, my blood turning to ice as I heard her tentative, "Hello?" Only silence greeted her, and when she repeated herself, the caller simply hung up without a word.

I was on tenterhooks, dreading each time the phone might ring again. Every unanswered moment fanned the flames of my anxiety, and soon the calls came more frequently, each one chipping away at my sense of safety until I hardly recognised myself.

Amidst that relentless fear, I clung to the normalcy of my part-time job at a hairdresser's—sweeping up and making tea. It was a harmless gig, a simple way to earn a bitof pocket money. And believe me, every penny felt like a lifeline. I was desperate to ditch my old Woolworths trainers—those trainers that reeked of discount regret and made me feel like a walking clearance rack. Earning even a few extra quid meant I could finally dream of apair of trainers that didn't scream "bargain bin." It was my little rebellion against a childhoodof budget footwear; every shift at the salon was a small step toward stepping out into something a bit more respectable.

But just as I began to savour those tiny victories, the terror crept back in. It was on that same job that the calls escalated, moving from the privacy of our home to impacting meat work as well. This man—whoever he was—found me there and started calling the salon, asking for me by name in a disturbingly intimate tone: "I saw you today. I know what you'rewearing."

During work hours, each ring made my stomach sink further. At that moment, the humour of earning pocket money faded, replaced by paralyzing fear. I began dreading even the thought of stepping outside, constantly looking over my shoulder, terrified that he might be lurking, watching, waiting for me somewhere.

Eventually, I couldn't bear the torment alone. I broke down and told my mum everything. Together, we went to the police. They listened, took my statement, and tried to reassure me, but it'd be years before technology could trace calls with any reliability. They warned us it wouldn't be easy to catch him.

The calls usually came early in the evening. The man insisted on meeting me, so the police concocted a plan—a trap if you will. I'll never forget that evening. It was around 6 or 7 p.m., and as the sky darkened, I was led to a quiet, isolated lane, flanked by plainclothes officers. I walked down that path, shaking uncontrollably. My hands were clenched so tightly that my nails dug into my palms, my chest felt heavy, and every shallow breath reminded me that I was utterly terrified. Every step was an eternity until I waited—and waited—but he never showed.

Yet the calls didn't stop. They continued relentlessly, and I found myself living in a perpetual state of dread. Thankfully, not long after, the house we lived in was sold. It had been on the market for a while, and when it finally sold, it felt like an escape. Moving house brought a slight reprieve. We made sure to go on ex-directory, so only a handful of people had our new number. And slowly, the calls ceased.

For a time, it was like a weight had been lifted from my chest. But the fear lingered—the nagging 'what if?' Who was he? Why me? Even now, I've never truly known. Perhaps it was a prank. As such, I have learned that over time, those fears fuse with more mature fears, and grow more complex but are just as powerful.

Looking back, that period was one of the most harrowing times of my life. As a child, I was consumed by fear, paranoia, and a deep sense of helplessness. The end of school should have brought relief, yet it only added another layer of pain.

In the big hall, we were gathered together as the teachers handed out praise like confetti. I recall them calling out names: "Well done, Stephen, you're going to go far! Peter, you'll be a rocket scientist one day!" Each name was followed by visions of a bright future.

And then they got to me. I waited with bated breath, desperate for something—anything—positive. Instead, they laughed and said, "You'll probably end up behind a bar . . . or working in McDonald's."

Cheers for that vote of confidence. Don't get me wrong—I love McDonald's as much as the next person—but that message was clear: I was a failure. That dismissal assumption has stuck with me all these years. I've carried that anger and frustration well into my teens and beyond. I often wondered, why couldn't I be a rocket scientist? Perhaps because I couldn't even spell it at the time. 'Scientist' is still one of those words that evades me. But the deeper pain was not the job itself—it was the belief that I wasn't worth investing in, that my future didn't matter.

Even now, it stings. It wasn't about the actual roles or careers; it was about the message that had been drilled into me— an assumption of inadequacy that I've had to fight against ever since.

CHAPTER THREE:

A Wild Step Forward

In my 20s, I began to figure out how to navigate the world—or so I thought. Even back in school, I had learned an important lesson: if I could make people happy or if I could make them laugh, they'd like me. And so, I became a people-pleaser, doing whatever it took to be accepted. But underneath it all, I had no confidence. None. So how could I pull it off?

That's when I found alcohol. It became my crutch, my magic elixir. When I drank, I felt alive. I wasn't just happy—I was unstoppable. Everyone seemed to love me when I was drinking. I was the fun one, the life of the party. But deep down, I knew the truth: I didn't have a clue who I really was. Alcohol gave me a confidence I couldn't find on my own.

When I was drunk, I felt great. But when the buzz faded, I'd crash hard—low, insecure, and uncertain.

So, I kept drinking. A lot. And when I say a lot, I mean it. I partied so much that the bouncers all knew me. I didn't even have to queue; I'd just stroll right in like I owned the place. Without alcohol, there was no way I'd have had that kind of nerve. But drinking gave me what I needed—or at least, what I thought I needed—to feel like I belonged.

I worked hard, but I played even harder. And let me tell you,

I did have fun. The '90s were electric, especially if you were part of the London club scene. Nights at Café de Paris, Browns, Stringfellows—it was pure magic. The music, the lights, the energy—every weekend was a new adventure and holidays abroad? They took the *fun* to a whole new level—dating!

Oh God, where do I even start? Dating—what a bloody nightmare. I've had my fair share of oopsie-daisy moments, but this one? Oh, this one takes the cake. It was quite possibly my most embarrassing date ever.

So, there I was, off on a date with a perfectly lovely man—sweet, fun, kind. The sort of man your mum would approve of. He picked me up and took me for dinner at this charming little pub. It was all going rather well—we chatted, laughed, and had a couple of glasses of wine. Very civilised.

Then, mid-giggle, he suggested we go for a little walk. WTF. What the hell am I doing? In theory, it sounded romantic—moonlit stroll, historic castle, all very fairy-tale-esque. But in reality? I was teetering in ridiculously high heels, the kind that scream sit still and look pretty, not hike across medieval ruins. But, not wanting to seem high-maintenance, I forced a smile and chirped, "Oh, that sounds lovely!"

But inside, I was thinking, Bloody Nora, I'm probably going to end up falling arse over tit.

We set off towards a nearby castle in Pevensey Bay—romantic, right? Except, my feet were killing me, and within minutes, I was sweating like a pig in August. Not quite the dreamy moonlit stroll I had envisioned. By the time we reached the castle, I was on the verge of collapse—and, even worse, I desperately needed a wee.

Now, here's where things took a turn for the dramatic.

I spotted a low stone wall that I thought we could climb over—you know, to get a better look at the castle. (Translation: I needed a bush. Urgently.) He was a bit hesitant—he had a sort of will from The Inbetweeners energy—but I convinced him.

Big mistake. HUGE.

The next thing I knew, I was screaming, tumbling through the air, and then—BOOM. I'd fallen. Fifteen feet. Into a bloody moat.

Yes. A moat.

At this point, a few things became alarmingly clear:

It was pitch black.

It was wet, cold, and full of God-knows-what. I still needed a wee.

Meanwhile, my date—who had wisely stayed on the right side of the wall—ran back to the pub to get help (as, in those days, we didn't have mobile phones. The dark ages, truly). So, there I was, alone in a 1,000-year-old moat, marinating in mud and historical regret.

The heels were ruined, too—marked and scraped. So not only was it a bad date with nearly broken bones, but I also ruined a lovely pair of heels! Every girl's nightmare!

After what felt like an eternity, flashing blue lights appeared. The police, fire brigade, AND an ambulance turned up. *Fantastic.*

A policeman leaned over the edge and called out, "Miss, are you alright?"

While lying flat on my back, soaking wet and humiliated, I shouted back, "WELL, I'VE BEEN BETTER."

They decided the best course of action was to lower a stretcher down on a winch. I was strapped in like some sort of medieval damsel-in-distress—except, instead of a handsome knight, I had a group of paramedics trying not to laugh.

As they hoisted me up, the policeman chuckled, "Miss Palmer, this castle has been here since 1066, and no one has ever fallen into it before. How long have you been here?"

"Oh, about two hours," I replied.

Cue roars of laughter from the entire rescue team. And as if things couldn't get worse—oh, they did.

I'd landed in such a way that my dress had ridden up spectacularly, revealing everything. Thankfully, that night, I had not chosen my 'lady garden week' knickers: HUGE pants. Small mercies.

Once at the hospital, I was wheeled straight to X-ray. But by now, my bladder was on fire. I begged the nurse to let me go, but no—protocol. So, they brought out one of those horrific tin commodes.

My poor date was behind the curtain. Bless him, he tried to give me some dignity.

But honestly, have you ever tried peeing into a metal bowl in absolute silence? The echo was mortifying.

At that point, I thought, *Sod it*. He's never going to see me again. May as well embrace the horror.

And you know what? He actually stuck around. He even said

it was the best date he'dever been on.

In hindsight, I think he was just relieved I didn't die.

But, needless to say, we didn't end up together. Can't imagine why.

Honestly, though—I just think some people are born clumsy. And unfortunately, I amone of them.

I couldn't wait to get back to work to tell the girls—they'd scream with laughter! Then came the job offer abroad. I jumped at the chance without hesitation. Back then, traveling wasn't as common as it is now—especially for someone like me. I'd been on a couple of holidays, but this was different. This was me, leaving everything behind for something completely unknown. People warned me with their usual clichés: "You're going to get the shits," they said. "You'll hate the food. You'll miss home." But I didn't care. I washungry for something new—a new vibe, new culture, new music, new food.

***

The moment I stepped off the plane, reality hit me. I was scared. I didn't know a single soulin this country. On the transfer to my hotel, I watched the barren landscape of America passby— dry, desolate, endless stretches of nothing. No houses, just rocks, and a few scattered trees. My chest tightened with every mile. Had I made a mistake? What was I doing here? The excitement that had carried me across the ocean started to dissolve into fear.

When I arrived at the hotel, they told me I'd stay there for a few days until someone would meet me and take me to work. I unpacked in silence, sitting on the edge of the bed, overwhelmed by the loneliness. No alcohol. No friends. No music. This wasn't the adventureI'd imagined. Where was the fun? The partying?

Hours passed, and I felt like I'd made the biggest mistake of my life. Then suddenly, there was a loud knock at the door. My heart jumped as I opened it, and standing there was a woman with the biggest, warmest smile I'd ever seen. "Hi! You're the newbie, right? We're all going out tonight. Want to come?"

Yes, please. That's all I could say, and that's when everything changed.

From that night on, it was freedom. Pure, unadulterated freedom. We danced until sunrise, laughed until our cheeks hurt, and partied like every night was the last. Work started at 9 a.m., finished at 6 p.m., and by 7 p.m., we were out again—drinks in hand, music pounding, and back home by 3 a.m. if we were lucky. It was wild, exhilarating, and completely unsustainable, but I didn't care. I was living the life I'd always dreamed of.

The job itself? Well, that was another story. I was supposed to be working in finance, but between the late nights and the endless partying, it quickly became clear that crunching numbers was not my calling. I struggled to keep up, and I could feel the weight of it all beginning to crush me. The girls in the office were fantastic, though—they made the days bearable. And my boss? She was something else.

One day, she called me into her office. My stomach dropped. I was terrified. Was this it? Was I about to be sent home? I wasn't ready to leave—I was having far too much fun. But instead of scolding me, she surprised me. She said, "This isn't working, is it? But I see potential in you. How about you give repping a try?"

Repping. I had no idea what that even meant, but I didn't hesitate. "Okay," I said. "Why not?"

That decision changed my life. It wasn't just a job—it was a crash course in people,resilience, and survival. It taught me skills I didn't even know I had. Organising, problem-solving, dealing with difficult customers, and working under pressure—shaped me in ways I'll always be grateful for. And most importantly, it gave me new-found confidence A kind of confidence I've never felt before.

Looking back, I realise that chapter of my life wasn't just about partying or escaping—it was about growth. I found parts of myself I didn't even know existed. And for the first time, I felt like I could take on anything.

I loved being a rep—it was so much fun, but it wasn't without its challenges. One of the first things they told me was that I'd have to run a welcome meeting for the new arrivals. A 45-minute talk about the island of Puerto Rico, the excursions, and anything else they needed to know. I remember walking into my first meeting, absolutely petrified. My stomach churned as I faced a sea of expectant faces, all staring up at me. I thought, What the hell have I done? How am I going to pull this off?

I hadn't even been on most of the excursions yet—unless you counted the bars. I vividly remember standing in Linkers Bar one night, one of the young Linkers family members walked in, smiled at me, and suddenly, I felt even more pressure to perform.

Standing there, completely sober, trying to act confident while everyone watched me . . . it was overwhelming. The good thing, though, was that people on holiday were generally happy. They were there to relax and have fun, and that worked in my favour.

I somehow stumbled my way through that first meeting. It felt like it lasted two hours instead of 45 minutes. I was awkward, nervous, and fumbling my words, but somehow, I made two sales. It wasn't much, but it was a start. You see, when I worked in finance, I had a set wage. But this job? It was all about commission. I didn't have much money, so I had to learn fast.

Over time, I started going on the excursions myself, studying the pattern and figuringout how to get better at selling. If I'd had a drink beforehand, I would've been fine—confident, even. But sober? It was tough. And then there were the difficult times.

I remember one particularly brutal stretch. We'd been partying hard—barely slept—and then it was straight to the airport to pick up new passengers. I'd find them, greetthem, and take them to their hotel. On the way, I'd give a speech on the bus, which wasn't too bad because I just had to read from a little script. But by the time I'd dropped everyone off, it would be 1 or 2 a.m. I'd get a few hours of sleep, and then it was straight back to the hotels to do the circuit again.

One morning, I'd dropped off a group at around 1 a.m. and went to visit them again at 11 a.m. When I walked into the reception, I was immediately surrounded by a group of 25 people—all screaming at me. I was only in my early 20s, and I had no idea how to handle it.

They were furious about the hotel, which was a basic three-star. It was exactly what they'dpaid for, but I quickly realised that wasn't what they were expecting. I just stood there, exhausted, in the height of summer heat, tears streaming down my face. They calmed down eventually, but it was a hard lesson: often, the angriest person in the group is the ringleader.If you can win them over, the rest will usually follow.

But the situation didn't get easier. On one occasion, a couple had paid for the mostbasic hotel option—so basic it didn't even have a proper reception. It was an 1830s accommodation, and let me tell you, it was as bare-bones as it gets. When I arrived, I was thereceptionist, the problem-solver, and everything in between.

I walked into the small reception area, and before I could even take a breath, a manwith a face like thunder stormed up to me. "What are you going to do about this?!" he shouted, his voice booming through the tiny room. I tried to explain that it was peak season,and there were no other accommodations available except for a five-star resort—which would cost extra. But he wasn't having it.

Before I knew it, he grabbed me by the throat and slammed me against the wall. I screamed, terrified, tears streaming down my face. I was shaking so badly I couldn't think straight. By some stroke of luck, a fellow rep happened to be walking past the reception. He was a big guy, and as soon as he heard me scream, he came running. He managed to pull the man off me, and I'll never forget the relief I felt at that moment. But the fear stayed with me.

That incident shook me to my core. I'd never been around that kind of aggression before, and it made me realise how vulnerable I was. After that, I started thinking about home more often—especially about my nan.

***

Life as a rep abroad in the late 90s was a relentless rollercoaster. You worked your fingers to the bone by day and partied even harder by night, swept up in a 24/7 whirlwind that never letyou forget you were far from home. Every evening was a blur of late-night gigs where Britpop anthems by Oasis and Blur, and pulsating beats from The Chemical Brothers and Massive Attack, provided the soundtrack to our escapades.

The 90s was an era defined by music that was raw, edgy, and

unmistakably vibrant—a constant reminder of the electric energy that pulsed through our veins. One songthat always takes me back to that time is Your Love by Frankie Knuckles. Every time I hear it, it brings back so many glorious memories of those days.

That endless cycle of work and play was a welcome distraction from the gnawing homesickness. Yet, on quiet nights, when the club lights dimmed and the music faded, I'd lieawake in my bed, utterly exhausted but unable to sleep. In those moments, the laughter and music couldn't drown out the memory of my nan, and I'd find myself haunted by thoughts of what I'd left behind.

About a year before I left England, my nan was diagnosed with cancer. She was my best friend, my rock, and leaving her was one of the hardest things I'd ever done. At first, she didn't tell us, but we started noticing the lumps around her neck. Eventually, when shebegan throwing up, she had no choice but to tell us the truth. That moment nearly broke me—she had always been there for me.

She went through chemotherapy and various treatments, losing her hair in the process. It was painful to see her like that, but over time, she started to get a little better.

Even from afar, she was always in my heart. We stayed in touch as much as we could—I called whenever I had the chance, and she wrote me letters. I can't tell you how much thoseletters meant to me. Opening one and seeing her handwriting made me smile, even on the toughest days.

During downtime, while repping, I missed my nan the most. Lying by the pool, myfirst thought was always of her. In a way, being a rep helped because I was constantly busy—there wasn't much time to dwell on things. But no matter where I was, she was always with me.

But one of the reasons I decided to go abroad was to get some distance—from my life, from everything, and, in part, from *him*. I had met someone a year or two before I left. He was fun, and kind, and we got on so well. We loved partying together, and eventually, I moved in with Bill, 200 miles away from home. I was homesick at first, but I started to adjust. I made new friends, found a job, and, for a while, it was just the two of us. We were like two peas in a pod—inseparable.

But then, as time went on, I started making more friends and going out with them too.

It felt good to have my own space, my own fun. One of the girls I became close with had connections with some rugby players from Bradford Bulls. I didn't know much about rugby, but they were a nice group of guys, friendly and fun to be around. We'd all hang out together, and one of them even liked me. He was handsome, but I was happy in my relationship—at least, that's what I kept telling myself.

As the months went on, cracks began to show. My boyfriend wanted it to just be the two of us, all the time. He didn't like me going out so much, especially with my friends and the rugby lads. I understood his perspective—seeing a group of rugby players at our house must have looked bad—but there was nothing to it. We were just having fun.

Still, his reaction made me feel trapped. I started to crave my freedom. I wanted to go out, to enjoy myself, to experience life. The more I partied and the more I went out, the more the gap between us widened. He wasn't unkind—far from it. He loved me deeply, but I was young, restless, and not ready to settle down.

Eventually, I left. I moved back home, hoping to regain some clarity. But Bill followed me. He declared his undying love, showed up wherever I was, and even sent a van full of flowers to my house. The florist said it was the largest order they'd ever seen for one person. I was overwhelmed. He was so kind, and so persistent, and I didn't have a bad word to say about him. But I couldn't handle it.

He was older than me and wanted to settle down, while I was just getting started. My nan's health was also worsening at the time. She'd been in and out of the hospital, and I wanted to be there for her. Despite everything, he kept coming back—every day off, every weekend. I told him it was too much, that I couldn't do this anymore, but he wouldn't stop. It wasn't just me he wouldn't leave alone. He started showing up at my nan's house, knocking on her door. My nan, being the kind and loving woman she was, tried to handle it at first. But she wasn't well, and eventually, it became too much for her. One day, she called me and asked if I could speak to him.

I tried again, begged him to leave her alone, to let me go. But he didn't stop. He'd hide in the village or park outside our house. Then came the moment I'll never forget.

My nan called my mum one day and said, "Can you get her to come round? He's sitting in the car on the drive." I drove over, heart pounding, and found him there, waiting. Crying, I pleaded with him to leave us alone. That's when he looked at me, calm but broken, and said he was going to kill himself. He had a hosepipe in his car and was completely serious.

I froze. I didn't know what to do or say. Inside, something told me he wouldn't go through with it, but the doubt and fear were still there. My head was spinning, my heart racing. Finally, in sheer panic, I said, "Oh, go on then," and drove off, shaking and feelingsick to my stomach.

I couldn't leave it like that, though. After a few minutes, I turned the car around and drove past quickly to see if he was still there. He was. I kept going, giving it another minute and drove by again. When I didn't see his car, my stomach dropped—I was ready to call thepolice and an ambulance. But just as panic set in, I realised he was gone. Relief washed over me, but I was trembling, my body tense, my head pounding. I sat in my car and cried, the weight of everything crashing down on me.

Looking back now, I can't help but think—how times have changed. The kind of lovethat once felt suffocating is the kind of love many would dream of today.

Weeks passed, and I didn't see Bill again. But by then, my nan had started to getbetter, and just when I thought I might catch my breath, I got the call to go abroad. It couldn't have come at a better time. I needed an escape. I needed to get away.

You see, going abroad was such an escape for me. It's funny, reflecting on it now, thatall of us who worked abroad were misfits in one way or another—running from something, hiding from something, or just searching for a way to feel free. We didn't talk about it openly, not in those days, but the cracks were always there, just beneath the surface.

Some of the people I hung out with were gay, but back then, that wasn't something you shouted from the rooftops. It was an unspoken truth, a quiet part of who they were. Oneof my closest friends was from Ireland, and he told me once, after a few drinks, that he couldn't ever truly be himself at home. It was too dangerous, too judged. But out there, under the Mediterranean sun, he could let loose. I'll never forget the sight of him, dancing to Kylie Minogue and Whitney Houston, twirling around my handbag, his face lit up with joy. Those moments were magic—pure, unfiltered freedom.

We were all hiding something in our own way. For some, it was their identity. For others, it was the weight of expectations or the pain of feeling unseen. We were a family of misfits, bound together by the unspoken understanding that we were each other's safe space.

It didn't matter who you were back home—out there, you belonged. We drank, we danced, we laughed until our stomachs ached. We didn't dwell on our problems; instead, we buried them under layers of fun and chaos. For a time, it worked.

But then everything came tumbling down.

***

One day, we went on a booze cruise. I always hated those trips because I got seasick, so my job was to meet and greet passengers when the boat docked. That day, one of the lads—Boy George, as we called him—was there. He was gorgeous, the kind of guy who made everyone's head turn. I liked him, but I'd been through too much to even entertain the idea of a boyfriend. I was perfectly happy with my little circle of gay best friends and girlfriends—they wanted nothing from me but fun, and I wanted nothing more than to keep things simple.

But Boy George was playful, always messing about, teasing in a harmless way. That day, in his usual cheeky manner, he picked me up and chucked me into the sea. It was all in good fun—no malice, just laughter—but the way I landed changed everything. My foot hit the sand awkwardly, and I felt an unbearable pain shoot up my leg. Snap. All my toes on one side of my foot were broken.

The air was blue as I screamed in agony. The pain was excruciating. I was rushed to the hospital, where they patched me up as best they could, but I couldn't walk. I was on crutches for six weeks, which was a nightmare because our hotels were perched up steep hills, connected by endless flights of stairs. Our daily routines required miles of walking between properties, and there was no way I could manage it.

The boys I worked with were amazing. They carried me down the stairs so I could still go out partying that week—bless them—but I couldn't do my job. Eventually, I had to go home. Boy George was devastated—he couldn't look at me or be around me. He felt so guilty, and it's funny how that changed him. He went into his shell for a while, which was so sad. I never blamed him. I know everyone was upset when I left. He had only been there a few months, and I think he struggled.

I didn't really get to say goodbye properly because he was on one side of the island, and we only saw everyone together once or twice a week—either at the booze cruise, the airport, or on a night off. It's such a shame because I really fancied him. He never meant to hurt me, and I knew at that moment that if he could have taken it back, he would have.

I hope he reads this, and I hope it never affected him. We didn't have Facebook or any social media back then—we didn't even use email with any regularity yet. It was all just starting to become a thing. No one had a way to contact me, and vice versa since I didn't even have a phone. After over a year of freedom, fun, and forming lifelong friendships, I returned to reality with a bump.

The culture shock hit me hard, but there was one thing I couldn't wait to do—see my nan. The first moment I saw her was bittersweet. She looked so small, so frail. She had always been my rock, my safe place, but now, it was like she needed me more than I neededher. It broke my heart to see her that way.

I spent every spare minute with her after I got back. We'd pour ourselves a little scotch, sit in her cosy living room, and I'd tell her all my stories. I'd recount the wild nights, the laughs, the ridiculous things we got up to abroad. She'd laugh with me, her eyes twinkling with that same warmth I'd known my whole life. In those moments, it was like nothing else mattered.

We had magic, my nan and me. Those evenings with her were some of the most precious moments of my life. It felt like the rest of the world melted away, leaving just the two of us, sharing stories and love. But as much as I cherished those times, there was a part of me that still ached for the freedom I'd found abroad, for the family of misfits who had given me a home when I needed one most.

CHAPTER FOUR:

Just As Everything Was Falling into Place,

He Walked In

I am actually crying as I write this. Over those last few weeks, my nan went downhill fast. Her cancer had pretty much spread throughout her whole body, but I sensed a lot of her emotional pain came from losing my grandad. I never met him, but I know how much my nan loved him. Loneliness had taken root inside her, festering with the same quiet cruelty as the disease that'd been consuming her body.

It's a memory that still haunts me. I can recall the way she'd speak about him, her voice soft and trembling as if each word was a precious relic of a past too painful to revisit.

Even though I never had the chance to meet him, the stories she shared were filled with warmth, laughter, and the kind of love that only seems to belong in the best of fairy tales. But as the cancer took hold, I could see that her grief had never fully healed—it was like a wound that time couldn't close. In her final days, that loss mingled with the unbearable physical pain, creating an agony that was as much emotional as it was corporeal.

It was so hard watching someone you love so much suffer

like that. It broke me in ways I'm not sure I fully understand even now. I remember her looking at me with tears in her eyes, her frail hands shaking as she reached out. "Lisa, please help me. I don't want to be here anymore. I'm in so much pain. Please help me." Her words echoed in my ears, reverberating through every quiet moment that followed. And I wanted to—God, I wanted to help her so badly. I knew she longed for an escape from the relentless torment of her body, but I was so helpless. It was like standing on the edge of a vast, dark chasm, looking down into a void I could neither reach nor fill. I was still in my 20s, with so little life experience to guide me through such profound loss and despair. What could I have done? Was there anything at all that I could have done to ease her suffering? Every question, every helpless thought, added to the crushing weight on my heart.

Back then, we didn't have Google or the ease of finding answers online like we do now. We'd just gotten a computer into the house, and even getting online was a maddening ordeal—the high-pitched screeches and whines of the dial-up connection still ring in my ears. I remember waiting impatiently for emails to download, the process so excruciatingly slow that I could have made a proper cup of tea and settled in with a biscuit before anything useful appeared on the screen. In that clunky, analogue era, the lack of quick access to information made everything feel even more isolated. I was left alone with my thoughts, and those thoughts were full of guilt and despair.

Even so, that memory of my nan begging me for help never left me. It's like a shadow that follows me, a lingering guilt that I carry every day. I often replay those moments in my mind, wondering if I could have been braver or if I could have offered her some relief. There she was, in so much pain, crying in agony, her frail body lying on two mattresses in a desperate attempt to ease her aching. Nothing seemed to help—not even the painkillers in the hospital, which only dulled the sensation for a little while before the pain returned with a vengeance. Yet, through it all, her mind stayed as sharp as a pin. It was as if even the cancer couldn't touch her intellect, even if it had ravaged her body.

Those weeks were some of the darkest of my life. I started feeling very low, sinking into a kind of despair that I hadn't known before. My nan was eventually moved into a hospice, a place where she spent about six or seven weeks before she finally passed away. I remember those weeks in excruciating detail—the sterile smells of the hospice, the constant beeping of machines, and the quiet, almost oppressive sadness that seemed to seep from the walls. Losing her nearly broke me. It felt like the safety net that had always been there, the one that caught me when life was too hard, had suddenly vanished. She wasn't just a relative; she was my best friend, my confidante. Who was I going to talk to now? We used to chat for hours about everything and nothing at all. Her laugh, her insights, her gentle way of understanding without judgment—it was all gone in an instant, leaving me with a hollow ache where love and security once resided.

I barely remember her funeral—perhaps because the pain was so overwhelming that my mind blocked out most of it. I do remember the slow procession, the damp chill in the air, and the sound of muffled voices as people gathered back at the house afterward. But I couldn't stand being around anyone; the weight of loss was too heavy. I slipped away on my own, seeking solace in solitude. I didn't want to talk or see anyone. Every face reminded me of what I'd lost, every word seemed trivial in the shadow of such profound grief.

I'd often find myself wandering through empty rooms, tracing my fingers over surfaces that still held the faint scent of her perfume. I'd linger in the silence of our shared spaces, hoping somehow that by holding on to these small, tangible remnants of her presence, I could stave off the insufferable loneliness. In those moments, I'd cry until my tears were dry, feeling the raw sting of regret and helplessness. I questioned everything—my choices, my inability to help her, the cruelty of fate that left her in so much pain.

It's strange how grief can make time stretch on endlessly. Some days, a single hour can feel like a lifetime, while on others, the hours slip by in a haze of numbness. On those days, I would sit by the window and while staring out at the grey, overcast sky, wonder if the rain was trying to wash away my sorrow. I remember feeling the cold bite of the wind on my face and thinking how it mirrored the chill that had settled in my heart. The physical pain of losing her was, in some ways, less agonising than the emotional void that followed.

I tried to keep myself busy—throwing myself into work, spending long hours with friends, and even attempting to pick up hobbies that once brought me joy. But nothing could quite fill the emptiness that her absence created. I remember evenings when I'd be surrounded by people, laughing and talking, yet feeling completely isolated as if I were invisible. It was as if the world had moved on, leaving me stranded in a limbo of memories and unspoken sorrow.

Sometimes, in the dead of night, when the world was silent and I lay awake, I'd imagine what it would have been like if she were still here. I'd think about her gentle smile, the way she'd always knew just what to say to make everything seem alright, even if only for a moment. I'd remember the sound of her voice telling me stories from her youth, tales of love and loss that seemed to carry the weight of a lifetime of experience. In those moments, the pain was almost bearable, softened by the bittersweet comfort of remembrance.

Looking back, I know that her final days were marked by a desperate need for release, a plea for mercy from a body and spirit both worn down by relentless suffering. And though I was too young, too unprepared to truly understand the depth of it all, I can now see that her pain was a culmination of years of loneliness, of living without the love and support she so desperately needed after losing my grandad. Her suffering wasn't just about the physical toll of cancer—it was also about the profound isolation that followed in its wake.

In the quiet moments of reflection that followed her passing, I often found myself questioning the nature of love and loss. How can one person's departure leave such an unfillable void? How can the absence of a loved one echo so loudly in every corner of your life? These questions, I suspect, are the same ones that keep others awake at night, pondering the cruel mysteries of existence, but sometimes, just when the darkness feels impenetrable, something—or someone—breaks through.

A few weeks after my nan passed, I went to bed around 10 p.m. as I had to work the next day. In the early hours, I felt something sit on my bed—it was strange, and it woke me up. When I looked to the end of the bed, my nan was sitting there. But she didn't look like she did at the end. She looked like she had twenty years earlier, before the cancer. She looked so well, so happy—and she was shining.

Despite Nan's pleasant demeanour, I've never been so scared in my life. I didn't believe in ghosts or spirits, and my mum and dad definitely didn't either. They were not spiritual people—very down-to-earth, practical, and sceptical about anything they couldn't see or explain. If I'd told them I'd seen Nan after she died, they wouldn't have laughed—theywould've said, "Don't be so stupid."

I hid under my duvet and told Nan to "go away, I'm scared." I was absolutely petrified, and I really regret that now, but it was incredibly frightening, and I didn't come out from under the covers until the morning, I was so terrified.

But now, I feel so blessed to have seen her— and to have seen her so happy.

It's been years since that painful time, but the memories remain as vivid as ever. Even now, when I catch a whiff of a familiar scent or see a photo of her smiling, there's a pang of sorrow mixed with gratitude for having known her. Grief is a complex, tangled emotion—one that doesn't simply fade away with time. It lingers, sometimes as a quiet ache, sometimes as a sudden, overwhelming wave of despair.

I have come to accept that some wounds never fully heal. They become a part of you, a reminder of what was lost, but also of the love that once was so incredibly strong. And while I wish I could have done more to ease her pain, I now understand that sometimes love means being there, even when you feel utterly powerless. It means holding onto the memories, cherishing the moments of warmth and laughter, and allowing yourself to feel thefull spectrum of emotions—even the ones that hurt the most.

I still find myself talking to her sometimes, whispering words of thanks and regret into the silence of the night as if by doing so, I could somehow bridge the gap between thisworld and hers. I tell her about my days, about the small victories and the ongoing battles with my own demons. And in those moments, I feel a connection that transcends the boundaries of life and death—a reminder that while she may be gone, the love we shared continues to light my way through the darkness.

As I write these words, tears continue to fall, not just for the pain of loss, but for the beauty of a life that touched mine so deeply. My nan's legacy is one of resilience, kindness, and an enduring love that will forever be a part of me. And though the grief remains a constant companion, I know that it is also a testament to the profound impact she had on my life—a reminder that even while suffering, love can shine through.

Her absence taught me that life is fleeting and that we must cherish every moment we have with those we love. It taught me to be brave in the face of unbearable pain, to seek solace in memories, and to find strength in the knowledge that love endures beyond the confines of this mortal existence. In the end, the scars of loss become a map of our journey—a testament to the battles we've fought and the love that carried us through.

I am still crying as I write these words, but with each tear, I feel a measure of release. I am learning to live with the pain, to honour her memory not by succumbing to despair, but by embracing the lessons she left behind. And though I know that the journey ahead will be long and fraught with challenges, I also know that her love will guide me, even in the darkest of times.

This is my story—a story of loss, of love, and of the unyielding strength that comes from facing our deepest fears. It is a reminder that even when life seems unbearably cruel, there is beauty in the memories, and hope in the knowledge that love, in its truest form, never truly dies.

In the months that followed, I went off the rails a bit. The grief was overwhelming, and I found myself drowning in it—turning to alcohol to numb the pain, seeking escape in a haze of drink and distraction. Then, as if life wanted to throw yet another curve, I was called up for jury service. Strangely, it turned out to be a blessing in disguise, even though my head was still a complete mess. It gave me something to focus on, a way to channel my turbulent emotions into something tangible.

Jury service was an experience I'll never forget. I know you're not meant to speak about it in detail, but the weight of having someone's life in your hands was both fascinating and terrifying. Sitting there, listening to the facts of a case, I felt a mixture of responsibility and dread. It was a constant struggle not to let my own inner turmoil seep into my judgment, yet the pressure was palpable. You try to remain impartial, suspend your natural instincts and view the situation with detached clarity, but the human element is impossible to erase. In those moments, when the opinions of others clashed with the facts presented, I found myself questioning everything—doubting my instincts, my values, and even my sense of self.

That period of service became a crucible for me. It forced me to confront the chaos within and, in a strange way, helped me start piecing together a semblance of order. Even though my heart was still aching from the loss of my nan, and the nights remained long and tear-filled, the experience of sitting in that courtroom, weighing the evidence of another person's fate, brought into sharp focus the importance of trust—trust in others, trust in the system, and most of all, trust in my own inner voice.

And yet, I often found that trust was elusive. Amid such intense pressure, my inner voice seemed to whisper doubts and uncertainties, echoing the same insecurity that had haunted me since those painful final days with my nan. I began to question whether I could ever truly believe in my own judgment, or if I was doomed to be swayed by the opinions and judgments of others. The experience of jury service, with all its moral and emotional complexities, was a stark reminder of just how fragile our inner resolve can be when faced with the weight of responsibility.

Despite the heaviness of those moments, there was a strange sense of liberation in being forced to make decisions that mattered—even if it was just in a courtroom setting. It was as if I was, in my own small way, reclaiming a part of myself that had been lost in the wake of grief and despair. Every verdict and discussion with fellow jurors, became a small step toward rebuilding the shattered pieces of my confidence. It wasn't a smooth process, and I still struggle to trust that inner voice, but I now see it as a journey—a difficult, winding path toward finding my own truth amidst the noise of the world.

Looking back, jury service wasn't just about fulfilling a civic duty; it was a turning point. It forced me to sit with the uncomfortable reality of life's complexities and, in doing so, helped me understand that healing isn't a linear process. Some days are marked by clarity and strength, while others are mired in doubt and sorrow. But each moment, no matter how painful, was a step on the path toward regaining control over my life.

In those moments of reflection, I realised that the experiences we endure—no matter how devastating or challenging—inevitably shape us. They leave us with scars, yes, but also with the wisdom and resilience to move forward. And so, while the loss of my nan and the ensuing spiral into self-destruction left me vulnerable, the experience of serving on that jury helped me start to rebuild a part of myself that I thought was lost forever.

That jury service taught me that even amid darkness, there is the possibility of light. It showed me that sometimes when we are forced to face the harshest realities, we also find the strength to confront our own inner demons. And slowly, with each passing day, I began to understand that while the echoes of grief might never fully fade, they can eventually give way to a newfound sense of purpose and hope.

After the first week of jury duty, a friend asked me to go out. I wasn't feeling up to it—every part of me screamed for solitude—but the girls wouldn't let it rest. One by one, all six of them rang me throughout the day, pleading, "You have to come out, please come!" I'd always been the life and soul of the party, loving every moment of going out, yet lately, an unfamiliar, heavy pit of sadness had taken up residence in my stomach. It was the strangest feeling I'd ever known, a deep melancholy that clashed with my usual exuberance. Finally, exhausted by their relentless pleas, I thought, "F**k it," and gave in. I went out, got absolutely pissed, and danced the night away, desperate to recapture that spark—even if just for a few fleeting hours.

At one point, I turned to the girls and said I needed the toilet. They came with me, and that's when John appeared—my first nightmare. He materialised out of nowhere, tall and magnetic, his presence impossible to ignore. For a split second, the chaos of the club faded into the background; the thumping bass and flashing lights dimmed as I locked eyes with him. He was handsome— breathtaking, really—and at that moment, I couldn't help but wonder, "Wow, who is this man?"

It felt like we talked for five seconds, though it was probably about five minutes—time warping around us as his confidence and easy charm enveloped me. His voice was soothing and resonant, like a scene straight out of a movie. But just as quickly as he'd entered my life, our taxi arrived, pulling me back to reality. Before I slipped away, he asked for my number, and I gave it to him almost in a trance, still reeling from that unexpected spark.

It's strange when I think about it now. The club wasn't even our usual spot—I'd never been comfortable there. It always gave me an uneasy feeling, as if something was slightly off. Looking back, I wish I'd paid more attention to that instinct. Perhaps if I had, things might've been different.

John texted me later that night, but I barely noticed; Sunday was a complete write-off.

I was absolutely hanging, nursing a hangover from hell, and with jury service looming on Monday, my phone was off-limits during the day, so his messages just waited. By midweek, however, he asked if he could pick me up that weekend and take me out. My first instinct was hesitation.

I hadn't dated in what felt like forever. My last relationship had left me scarred, and with everything that had happened with my nan, I was a shell of myself—lonely, heartbroken, and utterly lost. But also, I had the voice of my mum nagging in the back of my mind:

"You're not getting any younger—you'll be left on the shelf!" So, I suppose meeting up with John, when I really didn't even want to go out, was like ticking a box. Even if it was only for five minutes, it would make my mum happy. She was desperate for me to settle down.

Despite the swirling doubts and the knot of nerves in my stomach, I agreed.

The night of our date, I sat there staring at the clock, second-guessing every decision. I wasn't ready—God, I wasn't ready— but the loneliness was deafening, echoing in the empty spaces of my heart. So, before he even arrived, I cracked open a bottle of prosecco. By the time I heard his car pull up outside, half of it was already gone, its bubbles a temporary balm to my anxious soul.

We went out, had a few drinks, and laughed—a lot. He was charming, fun, and alwaysup for a good time, exactly my kind of person at that moment. I'd always been all or nothing: either I was out socialising, talking and laughing until my cheeks ached, or I was perfectly content at home with my animals, chilling or going for long walks. But back then, it was mostly socialising, and he seemed to enjoy that life just as much as I did.

Weekends together became a comforting routine—drinks, nights out, and laughter that momentarily filled the emptiness inside me. But then, slowly, little cracks began to show. I remember our second-ever phone call; he was in a foul mood because his car battery had died. It wasn't just a minor gripe—he was truly miserable, and that kind of misery clung to him like a shroud, draining every ounce of energy from those around him. I'm a glass-half-full kind of person, so I tried to cheer him up, to inject a bit of light into his dark mood. Looking back now, I realise just how much energy that took out of me. I hated seeing people upset, and I'd always do everything I could to make them happy—even if it meant sacrificing a bit of my own fragile stability.

At that moment, as I tried to bridge the gap between his despair and my own lingeringheartache, I felt the weight of my past all over again. The loss of my nan, the loneliness, thescars of failed relationships—all of it mingled with the thrill of new connection and the sting of self-doubt. And while I desperately wanted to hold onto the fleeting joy that John had brought into that night, I couldn't shake the nagging thought that maybe, just maybe, I wasn't ready to face these emotions head-on: to let someone in while my heart still ached over Nan's death, the pain sharpened by Mum's words: "You'll be the oldest swinger in town—just go!" Yet, despite the underlying tension and uncertainty, that night marked the beginning of a journey—a tentative step towards rediscovering parts of myself I thought were lost forever. It was a night of contradictions: of laughter amid lingering sorrow, of hope entwined with hesitation. And as I look back on it now, I see it not just as a night out, but as a fragile thread of light in a time when I needed it most.

You see, when you're in a relationship—whether romantic or even just a work relationship—the red flags are always there. We just choose to ignore them, brushing off the little things as if they were nothing. But those little things, over time, don't remain little; they grow, fester, and eventually become impossible to ignore.

***

A few months into John and I's relationship, life took an unexpected turn—I found out I was pregnant. My emotions swung wildly between sheer panic and a fragile sense of happiness. One moment, I was overwhelmed by terror, thinking, *I can barely take care of myself, how on earth am I going to raise a baby?* And then, in the next breath, a spark of joy flickered within me. It was a double-edged sword—a potent mix of hope and dread that left me questioning every decision I'd ever made. In that whirlwind of conflicting feelings, John decided to move to the quiet countryside of Surrey to be with me. I still had a good job, so we managed to find a flat together—a fresh start, or so I hoped. That's when the subtle shifts began.

At first, the changes were almost imperceptible. We'd go out together, and since I couldn't *drink*, I'd have just one glass of wine—a fragile attempt to partake in the social rituals that had once defined our nights out. But after a while, I started noticing things: the way he acted, the offhand comments that seemed too pointed, the small criticisms that crept into our conversations like unwelcome guests. I remember sitting there with a growing unease, thinking, *what have I done?* I was pregnant, and already, I had this sinking feeling in the pit of my stomach—a dreadful premonition that things weren't going to work out the way I had once imagined. And yet, I convinced myself that it would be fine. After all, from a young age, we're fed the fantasy of that perfect life—two kids, a white picket fence, everything falling into place. I clung to that vision, even as doubt seeped into every corner of my mind.

But then it got worse.

It began over something as trivial as a Diet Coke. I'd buy one—just one can—each day. And bearing in mind that I was bringing in most of the money at that point, I thought nothing of it. But then he started asking, almost interrogating me, "How much was that can of Diet Coke?"

I'd shrug and say, "A pound or something," trying to sound nonchalant. But then his tone would change—suddenly, it was as if that single can was an offense of monumental proportions.

He'd launch into a tirade about how I "shouldn't be drinking that" because "it all adds up."

I'd think, *What the hell?* Yet outwardly, I just nodded, desperate for peace, eager to avoid any argument that might shatter the fragile calm I was trying so hard to maintain.

And then it wasn't just about drinks—it was about food, where I went, and every small aspect of my day-to-day life.

Some evenings, after work, I'd stop by the pub for an hour—

just one hour—to catch up with friends. My job was isolating, and that little bit of social time was a rare luxury. But he would call, his voice edged with irritation, "Where are you?" Even if I was just in the pub, only for an hour, his words would slice through the merriment. "I'll walk down and meet you now," he'd add, as if my simple desire for a brief reprieve was a personal affront. I didn't fully grasp it then, but those were the first subtle hints of control creeping in—insidious and steady, until one day, they became the norm.

Every little criticism, every seemingly innocent question, built up day by day until I started questioning my own decisions. I was pregnant, so I told myself it was just stress and hormones, and that maybe I was overreacting. I made excuses for his behaviour, hoping that it was a phase that would pass. But deep down, a small, yet persistent voice told me that something was terribly wrong.

And then came the night my baby was coming. The fear hit me like a runaway train. I can still recall the moment vividly—the pounding in my chest so intense it felt as if an elephant were stomping inside, the sweat pouring down my face, and a nauseous terror that rendered me almost speechless. Amid that overwhelming pain, I found myself silently pleading. *Can we reverse this? Can I just NOT have a baby tonight?* I was two weeks overdue, and every passing minute on the drive to the hospital felt like torture.

I remember the excruciating moments in the car: "Drive faster!" and then, "No, drive slower!" as if my very life depended on it. I was the worst passenger in existence, my shouts and pleas mingling with cries of agony. The pain was so horrific that nothing could ease it—not even the sound of a soothing voice or the gentle touch of a hand.

When we finally arrived at the hospital, the ward was packed—typical, I suppose.

They asked if I wanted pain relief. "Yes, I'll take everything you've got!" I yelled, desperate for any respite. But I was already too far gone for anything other than gas and air. I must have screamed through the entire hospital corridor. If you're a man reading this, try to imagine squeezing a melon out of your backside—without any pain relief. I was a mess.

The gas hit me in waves—one minute I was giggling uncontrollably, the next I was shrieking in agony. At one point, a nurse came in and, with as much politeness as she could muster, she asked if I could "scream a little less loudly." I wanted to shout, "No, bloody hell, it hurts!" But the pain swallowed all my words.

I went through an entire bottle of gas before they had to switch it out for another, and then, to top it all off, I threw up—spectacularly, in a way that I wouldn't wish on my worst enemy. Hours passed, and still, the baby hadn't come. I was utterly exhausted, my body and mind frayed to the limits of endurance. And then, suddenly, everything changed—the monitors began to beep urgently.

"The baby's breathing has slowed. Your baby needs to come out now," someone announced, and a team of doctors rushed in. Fear clutched at my throat, and despite my fatigue, I no longer cared about anything but the safety of my child.

"Do whatever you have to do—just get my baby out safely," I pleaded, my voice raw with desperation.

Funny, isn't it? At the start of labour, you're so guarded about your privacy that you'd never let anyone see you in your most vulnerable state. By the end, however, you couldn't give a single damn about exposing everything—all you wanted was for your baby to be out. And finally, after what stretched into an eternity of pain and anxiety, they pulled my baby out.

For a moment, there was a deadly silence. I couldn't hear a cry. My heart stopped, and I was gripped by crippling panic. They rushed our baby into another room, and I lay there, paralyzed with fear, each second stretching into an eternity. And then—at last—they came back.

"You have a healthy baby boy."

In that instant, relief flooded through me, as if the dam of despair had been burst open. I was so happy. This was it. This moment, this tiny, fragile life, would somehow make everything work. We'd be a happy family, wouldn't we?

The first year was a blur—a whirlwind of night feeds, endless nappy changes, and exhaustion so deep it felt like I was drowning. Every time the house fell silent, my heart would lurch with fear. I'd rush over to his cot, holding a mirror up to his tiny nose, desperate to see that faint mist of breath and reassure myself that he was still there, still alive. The fear, that ever-present, nagging worry, never truly left me.

It took me a long while to fall in love with him in the way that everyone talks about—the instant, overwhelming bond as if a magical wave of devotion had washed over me. Of course, I knew I loved him; I always knew that deep down. But I expected to be hit by an immediate, fierce, all-consuming adoration. Instead, I felt doubt. *What's wrong with me?* I wondered, feeling as though I was failing at the very essence of motherhood. Why wasn't I that picture-perfect mum—the one with a tambourine in one hand and a bag of carrot sticks in the other?

Yet, I resolved to be the best mum I could be. I wanted to be the fun one, the kind one, the one who would tell my son the truth about the world instead of wrapping him in a bubble of overprotection. I wanted him to know that life was messy, unpredictable, and sometimes painful—but that it was also beautiful and full of wonder. Was that so wrong? At least, I thought, then he'd grow up knowing the truth about love, resilience, and the bittersweet nature of life.

I did the night feeds. When my son woke up in the early hours, I'd tend to him, my heart heavy with both love and exhaustion. During the day, I'd steal every spare minute to catch an hour's sleep before heading off to work in the evenings. But he seemingly hated it when I left.

And then, one day, something shifted. It had been slow at first, but then all at once, the wall I had built around my heart crumbled. Our bond became unbreakable, a fragile thread had woven itself into something strong and comforting. The guilt I'd carried for weeks—guilt for the doubts, for the fear, for not feeling that instantaneous, overwhelming love—melted away like ice under the morning sun. My love for my son grew stronger with each passing day, an encouraging reminder of the resilience of the human heart.

As time marched on and my son grew, whenever I walked out the door, I could see the hurt in his little eyes, the silent plea for me to stay. And each time, my heart shattered a little more. But we needed the money—we had bills to pay, and I had no choice but to keep the wheel turning.

I've come to realise that every twist and turn in that tumultuous period taught me something invaluable about love and loss. I learned that red flags, no matter how small, have a way of growing into something that can't be ignored. And even when you try to brush themaside, they have a way of resurfacing with a vengeance. Yet, amidst the heartbreak and the pain, there's beauty. There's beauty in the resilience of the human spirit, in the way we can rebuild even after the most devastating of losses, and in the quiet, steady growth of love.

Even if it doesn't burst forth like a tidal wave, but builds slowly, it can still become thefoundation of our lives.

Tension at home started creeping in like a slow poison. The moment John walked through the door, I'd tense up, my nerves straining to detect the slightest hint of his mood. I'dbrace myself: would tonight be one of the good nights, where he ate his dinner quietly, retreated to the shed to work out, and left us in peace? Or would it be one of the bad ones, thekind where every word was laced with venom? I never knew which version of him I'd be facing, and that uncertainty forced me to walk on eggshells every single day.

I tried to carve out moments of escape for both of us. I'd take my son on long bike rides—hours spent in the fresh air, just the two of us away from the stifling tension at home. I'd invite him to join us, hoping to create a little haven of normality. Sometimes, I even felt abittersweet relief when he chose to stay behind because when he was in one of his moods, theentire house would become a suffocating chamber of anger and resentment.

Money became his obsession—a tool of control that he wielded with precision. Every penny I spent was scrutinised as though it were a sin. I was given a fixed monthly allowance for food and petrol, and I clung to it as if my survival depended on it. But if I ever forgot something essential—like butter for the week—and had to dash back to the shop, that was the spark that ignited his fury. It wasn't just a minor annoyance; it was a trigger for a storm of screaming, relentless accusations that left me trembling. And yet, when he wanted something—when he fancied a gamble or a luxury—the rules suddenly changed, as if his desires were above reproach.

The shouting grew worse over time, the tension in our home thickening to an almost intolerable density. At least twice a week, I'd end up in tears, my body shaking with the silent cry of my soul. I never found the strength to stand up for myself; all I ever wanted was peace—a simple, quiet existence free from the constant barrage of criticism and control.

As the years passed, I felt myself slipping away. I lost sight of who I was beneath the layers of exhaustion and self-doubt. My job was stressful—a relentless grind that barely left me a moment to breathe. I'd rush to drop my son at school and then speed off to work—a thirty-minute drive squeezed into a twenty-minute window. I'd endure a full day of seven hours with no proper lunch break, all just to ensure I could be there to pick him up again.

Then came the endless cycle at home: cooking, cleaning, and trying to be the best mother I could for my little boy, who remained the only bright spot in my otherwise dark world.

And then he'd come home. Immediately, he'd dive into his routine of control: straight to the computer, scrutinising every bank statement, every expense. If I spent even a couple of pounds on something we truly needed—like bread for his sandwiches—it was as if I had committed an unforgivable crime. He'd explode, his anger spilling over as he would storm outside to check the car, his voice echoing in the night:

"Why have you done 36 miles? Work is 32 miles."

"I took our son to the park. It's two miles away. He loves the big slides there."

That was enough to set him off, and it became a nightly ritual—a monotonous cycle of control and indignation that seemed like Groundhog Day. Every single night, the same accusations, the same pattern of criticism and wrath, until I no longer recognised the woman I had been. I became a ghost of myself, lost in the labyrinth of his demands and my own desperation to keep the peace.

Then one evening, in the midst of this inescapable routine, my son looked up at me with sad, wide eyes and whispered, "Mum, can we just go? Let's leave." That simple, heartfelt plea hit me like a freight train. At that moment, I realised the full cost of living in a prison of constant fear and control—not just for me, but for my innocent child who deserved a life free from such terror.

A few weeks later, with trembling determination, I told John I was leaving. Instead of concern or sorrow, he laughed in my face, his laughter as cold and dismissive as his words:

"You'll never go. You've got nowhere to go. No one will have you. You'll never leave me."

And at that moment, he was right. I had nowhere to go—no money, no support, nothing but the chains of his control. Being with a narcissist like him was like walking oneggshells every day. You're constantly second-guessing yourself, wondering if a simple action will set off a chain reaction of anger and abuse. Every word, every decision was scrutinised, and you lived in perpetual fear of making the wrong move. It was an existence defined by constant anxiety, where the slightest misstep could shatter the fragile illusion ofnormality.

Looking back now, I can see how his controlling behaviour eroded not only my sense of self but also the joy that once filled my life. The relentless criticism, the micromanagement of every expense, and the unpredictable bursts of anger—all of it left scars that I still carry.

Yet, even in those dark moments, I held onto a sliver of hope—a hope that one day, I'd reclaim my life, rediscover my identity, and finally break free from the suffocating grip of his narcissism.

This is my story of losing myself, of feeling trapped in a life that wasn't mine to live. It's a story of how love, when twisted by control and narcissism, can become a prison. And it's a reminder to anyone who's ever felt that way: you deserve to live freely, to be respected, and to find a life where your worth isn't measured by someone else's controlling standards. I learnt that the first step to reclaiming yourself is recognising that you are worthy of more—a truth that, no matter how deeply buried under the weight of abuse, can always be unearthed with time, courage, and a little bit of hope.

***

The Picture That Changed Everything.

The years dragged on, each day a slow, painful march until one day my son came home from school with a drawing. I still remember that moment as if it were yesterday—it haunted me in a way I can scarcely put into words.

In the drawing, his dad was depicted standing with a beer can in one hand and a punchbag in the other, a crude attempt at capturing his essence. Beside him, my son had drawn himself, small and forlorn, his eyes brimming with sadness. And then there was me—drawn even smaller, with eyes that held a depth of sorrow and resignation I had never seen before. The words scrawled underneath sent a chill down my spine:

I wish my dad would drink more beer to make him happy and punch the bag instead of being angry. I wish there was a pill to make Mum happy again.

In one innocent, unfiltered piece of art, my son had voiced the unspoken truth of our home. In that single moment, I realised I couldn't do this to him. I couldn't continue living in a world where his only solace was to escape into these grim fantasies. It was the moment that shattered the numbness and forced me to confront the reality I had been too afraid to face.

It took months to work up the courage to leave, to break free from the grip of the life that had slowly strangled my soul. My mind was a chaotic mess, torn between paralyzing fear and a fragile glimmer of hope. But I knew deep down that I had to leave—not just for me, but for my son. And then, as if fate were toying with me further, we received the news: his dad had cancer. It hit me like a punch to the stomach, a cruel twist of fate that left me reeling.

I had always liked his dad—we'd gotten on well in the early days, and there was a time when we shared laughter and dreams of a future together. But now, despite the sadness that came with the news, I felt even more trapped. How could I possibly leave when the man, flawed as he was, now needed me even more? The very thought of abandoning him in his time of need twisted my insides, binding me to him with guilt and obligation.

I supported John as best as I could, trying to maintain a semblance of normality. But nothing changed. The eggshells beneath my feet grew sharper with each passing day. The mood swings, the shouting, the constant scrutiny—whether it was over bank balances, car mileage, or even the smallest expenditure—never ceased. It was as if every aspect of my life was subject to his relentless, invasive control.

***

Cracks in the Foundation.

Not long afterward we moved. The flat had served its purpose, but in the sweltering summer heat, it'd begun to feel more like a prison than a home. No garden, no space to breathe—just walls closing in on us. Moving evoked a fresh start, a chance to leave behind the memories of confinement and the echoes of past doubts. It was as though this new chapter would finally allow everything to fall into place, bringing with it the promise of a brighter, more hopeful future.

We moved while naively thinking that a fresh start in a new place might ease the mounting pressure and allow us both to breathe a little easier. We packed our belongings and moved house, all the while shuttling back and forth to see his dad, whose condition was deteriorating. Those journeys were nothing short of hell. On what should have been moments of shared grief and support, John's temper would flare up, and the two-hour drive became a battleground of angry shouts. I'd stare out of the window, trying desperately to block out his seething words, but they hit me like stones, leaving bruises that no one could ever see. I'd fight back tears, only to hear my son's quiet sobs from the backseat, a sound that shattered whatever composure I had left.

But I rode out the storm as best as I could, enduring each day and each night, clinging to the hope that someday I'd be free. Most nights, I would curl up next to my son, reading to him until he fell asleep, trying to shield him from the chaos that surrounded us. But going to bed with John became a torment in itself. The very thought of lying next to him made my skin crawl. I loathed him with every fibre of my being. The anger inside me was a constant, gnawing pain as if something was clawing at my chest, desperate to break free.

I scraped together every bit of money I could, sold things I'd once treasured, and saved for a holiday—a brief escape, a momentary respite from the oppressive weight of our lives. My son's seventh birthday was approaching, and I hoped that a change of scenery might lift the burden off our shoulders, even if just for a little while.

When I told John about the holiday, his reaction was immediate and furious. "We're not going. Just get a refund," he snarled. I couldn't believe it. My son, so full of excitement at the prospect of his first holiday—a break he'd looked forward to for months—broke down in tears right then and there. His innocent sobs, filled with disappointment and longing, tore at me.

I held him tight and whispered, "If it's the last thing I do, you and I are going on this holiday. No matter what. Don't worry." That night, with a trembling voice, I went downstairs and told John outright, "We are going. That's it."

He smirked, dismissive and cold. "No, you're not. And neither am I." I was shaking, a mixture of fear and newfound defiance coursing through me. For the first time in years, I had stood up for myself.

But the closer the holiday approached, the nastier his demeanour became. "I'm too busy. I can't go away. You're being selfish," he would bark. I ignored him, and a week before our departure, I packed our bags. He refused to go, so he was left behind, stewing in his own misery.

Our holiday was heaven. Eight blissful hours each day in the pool, my son's laughter ringing out like music, a birthday cake and celebrations that brought a sparkle back into his eyes. I waited for a call, a message from John—something to let me know he was there, perhaps missing us, or even just acknowledging our escape. But there was nothing. His silence was profound. The funny thing was, he had no work that week— he could have come. But he chose not to. And I didn't care. For the first time in years, I felt free. It was as if I had shed a 20-stone block of cement off my shoulders. There was no more moaning, no more controlling, no more walking on eggshells—just me, my son, and a taste of happiness.

Yet, as the holiday drew to a close, a dread settled over me. The thought of going back to that life made my stomach twist in knots. I didn't want to return—not for me, and certainly not for my son. The night before we were due to come home, I lay awake staring at the ceiling, my mind racing with the fear that I couldn't endure much more of that toxic existence.

The Picture That Changed Everything and the Cracks in the Foundation had been the tipping points—moments when I realised that the controlling, narcissistic love I'd been subjected to was not a normal part of life. It was a prison. And every day spent under that roof, every shout, every whispered criticism, eroded my sense of self until I was barely recognisable in the mirror.

This is my story—a story of humiliation, of endless anxiety and fear, of moments so raw and painful they still make me cry. It's the story of a woman who lost herself in the maze of control and manipulation, who lived on constant eggshells, wondering if every little move would set off a chain reaction of abuse. And it's a story of hope—when I finally gathered the strength to say,

"Enough." When I realised that I was worthy of a life free from terror, a life where I could be the person I once was, and the person I've longed to be.

I share this with you not to garner sympathy, but as a reminder to anyone who feels trapped in a cycle of control and humiliation: you deserve to live freely, to be respected, andto find joy in the simple moments of life. There is strength in recognising your worth, even when the world around you tries to convince you otherwise. And sometimes, the first step to reclaiming your life is simply believing that you are worth more than the chains that bind you.

***

When we got home that evening, John was quiet. Not grumpy, not angry—just silent. For a moment, I thought, has he realised? Has he finally seen what he's doing? But by the next day, he was back to his usual self, as if the silence had been nothing more than a brief pause in hisendless cycle of control.

A few days later, a neighbour I knew from school came around. Usually, she was fullof energy and always chatting away, but that day, she was in tears—something personal hadhappened, and she just needed someone to listen. I beckoned her inside and said, "Come in, let me make you a drink. We'll figure it out together." She stayed for about an hour and twenty minutes, crying and pouring her heart out, while my phone kept flashing with messages demanding that she leave. I could hear him pacing, huffing and sighing, growing more and more irritated— he hated having people around.

It was strange, really. When we first met, he had been the life of the party, always eager to go out, always charming. But after our son was born, everything changed. Friends who once meant so much became unwelcome intrusions; he made excuse after excuse to shut them out. And if anyone dared to turn up unexpectedly, his fury would bubble to the surface, masked by a fake smile that couldn't quite hide the venom beneath. I remember attending a BBQ once—feeling a flicker of excitement that maybe things might be different, more relaxed. Then, as I was helping bring out chairs, he grabbed my arm and hissed, "Make an excuse. We're leaving."

I saw the shock on my friend's face as she realised the mask was slipping, and people began to see the true nature of the man I was living with—a man who could be charming in public, yet transformed at home into a cold, controlling narcissist.

I was at breaking point.

Months blurred into weeks. Then, his dad passed away—a loss that shattered me completely. I had truly loved his dad, and I was a wreck at the funeral. Yet, even after that devastating blow, things only grew worse at home. I convinced myself to stay: another month, another week, another day of the same oppressive routine.

Then Christmas came. I tried to make it special—I cooked dinner, wrapped presents, and even managed to light up our son's face with the sparkle of the decorated tree. But John was as far removed from the festive spirit as ever. He went off to lift weights, forcing me to call out, "Dinner's ready."

He sat down, took one bite, and then spat it out. "What is this shit?" he roared before picking up his plate and smashing it across the floor.

My son burst into tears, and at that moment, Christmas—the day that should have been filled with joy, family, and love—was reduced to shattered plates and a suffocating gloom.

Later, a neighbour asked, "Lisa, are you okay? I heard noises last night." I lied through gritted teeth, "Yeah, it's fine." But it wasn't fine.

Months passed, and summer came and went. One day, I felt so ill I could barely move.

The head pains were so intense I feared I might collapse. My mum called the doctor, and even our neighbour came around to check on me.

"It's stress," the doctor said simply, and I knew deep down that if I didn't leave, I would never be happy again.

The holiday, the neighbour's visit, the constant tension at home—they all converged to make one thing clear: I had to leave. The road ahead was uncertain and fraught with fear, but I knew that if I stayed any longer, neither I nor my son would ever truly be free.

And so, with every ounce of courage I could muster, I began to plan for a new life—a life where the chains of control would no longer hold me down.

A few months later, I finally found the courage. I left him a note. I should have told him to his face, but the fear had been too overwhelming, and I was too scared to confront him directly. In the note, I wrote:

I'm leaving.

My phone will be off for a few days. We are safe.

I will never stop you from seeing our son, but I will not be speaking to you until things calm down.

It's not you, it's me.

I knew that last line was pure bullshit—a feeble attempt to soften the blow—but I clung to it anyway. And then, with trembling hands and a racing heart, I walked away.

For the first time in years, I was free.

CHAPTER FIVE:

Nowhere to Go, but Free

So, there we were—bags stuffed with clothes, a bin bag full of my son's toys, £250 incash, and a cheese and pickle sandwich wrapped in cling film. That was it. That was everything we had to our names.

I should have felt elated, triumphant even. After all those years of fear, of doubt, ofwalking on eggshells, I had finally done it. I had built up the courage to leave, and for a fleeting moment, I was proud of myself. But then it hit me.

Where on earth were we going to go?

Reality came crashing down like a tidal wave. I had no home, no real plan—just a carfull of belongings and a desperate need to escape. I had asked my mum if we could stay with her, but she hesitated. "You know what your dad's like . . . You need to work it out. You andhe don't get on," she said. And she was right. My dad and I had never been close. We barely spoke, and when we did, it was stiff and awkward—as if two strangers were trying to find common ground. Asking him for help felt impossible.

So that was it. No backup plan. No safety net. Just me, my son, and the open road.

I had to make it exciting for him. He didn't yet know we had left—not properly, notyet. I put on my brightest smile and said, "We're going on an adventure!" I forced my voice to sound cheerful, even as my heart hammered against my ribs.

He grinned and clapped his hands. "An adventure, he repeated."

I had no idea where I was driving, only that I had to keep moving. If I stopped, I might break, and if I overthought it, the fear would swallow me whole. I drove to the seaside—it was the only place that made sense. The sea had always been my safe space, aplace where the waves carried away my worries, even if just for a little while.

"Right," I said, trying to sound upbeat, "Let's find a B&B and have some fun!"

We found a cheap little guesthouse, its sign flickering in the dimming light. It smelled of old carpets and salt air, but it didn't matter—it was somewhere. We grabbed chips from a battered little chippy on the pier and sat by the arcade. My son giggled as he pushed pennies into the slot machines, completely unaware of the storm raging inside me.

I was trying to keep it together, to act normal, but inside, I was drowning. What thehell had I done? Where were we going to go? I had broken free from prison, only to feel adrift. Where would we build a new life? The weight of it pressed on my chest, tightening,suffocating.

Later, when we got back to the car to drive to the B&B, I got him in the back seat andsat beside him. My hands trembled as I took his little hands in mine.

"I have something to tell you," I began, swallowing hard

against the lump in my throat.

His wide, innocent eyes stared up at me.

"None of this is your fault, my love. But I . . . I can't live with your dad anymore." His brow furrowed slightly, but he didn't say anything. "I want you to know that I will never stop you from seeing your dad. You will always have him in your life—you'll still see him, you'll still see everyone, and you'll go to the same school. Nothing else has to change, I promise. But I just . . . I can't live with him anymore."

I braced myself for questions, for tears, for panic. But he simply nodded.

"Okay, Mum."

That was it. No anger, no fear—just a quiet, brave understanding. I pulled my son into my arms, and my body shook as I held him tight.

"Come on then, let's go back to the B&B and watch a film."

And we did—just me and my boy, starting the first night of our new life.

We stayed another night at the B&B, but I knew time was slipping through my fingers like sand in a broken hourglass. Money was running out—fast. I needed to get my life together and quickly. The reality of what I'd done was pressing down on me like a lead weight. I had escaped, but escape wasn't enough— I had to survive. We had to survive.

What on earth was I going to do?

For a while, we sofa-surfed, hopping between friends' places. I always felt like a burden, an intruder. They were kind and genuinely grateful for my presence, but I could see the pity in their eyes, the awkward glances when I stayed too long. That wasn't going to beenough.

Desperation forced my hand. I swallowed my pride and asked someone for help—just something to keep us going. I borrowed £600, the most money I'd had in my hands in a long time, and I used it to buy a mobile caravan. Not a cosy, Instagram-worthy home-on-wheels—no, it was a wreck. Damp, dirty, and reeking of mould that had seeped into its very walls. There was no carpet, just ice-cold metal underfoot. The walls were as thin as a baked bean tin, barely keeping out the creeping October chill, and the windows let in more draught than light. The entire place felt abandoned and forgotten by the world.

I spent weeks scrubbing it, painting over the filth, trying to turn it into something liveable. I did my best to lay some carpet and flooring, but if you've ever tried to use a Stanley knife without knowing what you're doing, you'd understand—I butchered it, leaving jagged cuts and holes that I tried to hide under a chair. I tried to make things nice for my son, to create a home from nothing. There was no working toilet, only a bucket—a cold, disgusting bucket in the centre of what was supposed to be our home.

And the nights? The nights were the worst. As darkness crept in, so did the freezing air, wrapping itself around us like icy fingers and seeping into every crack and gap. The caravan was akin to a metal coffin, trapping the cold and sucking the warmth right out of us.

I tried to find work—any work—but it was a joke. Every job application came with endless bloody questionnaires: tick this, rate that, select the "most accurate response." I was dyslexic, and I struggled. I knew that if they met me and saw my determination, they might give me a chance—but I couldn't even get my foot in the door. I had no money, and no way forward. With each passing day, I sank further into a darkness I couldn't shake. I forced a smile for my son, but inside, I was dying.

Christmas was the hardest. I felt the crushing pressure of not being able to buy my son a present. I was overcome with a sense of failure. What kind of mother doesn't give her child a gift?

My thoughts started to spiral—growing darker and heavier. I was slipping, and I didn't know how to pull myself back.

My son stayed with family for two nights—two nights when I should have rested, planned, and sorted my life out. Instead, I unravelled. One bitterly cold night, I stepped outside to use the bucket, shivering as my breath turned to mist in the air. And that's when it hit me. What am I doing? I was living like an animal. My son deserved better. Maybe he'd be better off without me.

That poisonous thought slithered into my mind and curled around my soul. I sat in that freezing caravan, the weight of failure crushing me. Guilt consumed me. I wasn't enough. I wasn't a good mother. I wasn't strong enough. I was nothing. Tears streamed down my face as I fell apart, silent screams trapped in my throat. It felt as if something evil was in the room with me, whispering all the worst things I had ever believed about myself. I was a failure. I was worthless. I was never going to make it.

And then, in that darkest moment, I gave in. I couldn't see a way out. Everything was black, endless, and suffocating. I didn't want to wake up tomorrow. I wouldn't have to feel this ache, wouldn't have to fight a battle I was sure I'd never win. I tipped the pills into my shaking palm, the small capsules rattling like tiny promises of escape. They stared back at me, offering relief, silence—an end to it all.

I sat there, staring at them, feeling a strange sort of calm settle over me. This was it.

The end. I could finally sleep—I was so tired, mentally and physically exhausted. The silence after the storm. But then—something happened.

A bolt of energy, a flash of light, a presence—I don't know what it was—but it stopped me. I didn't hear it, but I felt it, like a white-hot surge of electricity slicing through the darkness. For a moment, time seemed to freeze. My breath caught in my throat; and my heart pounded so violently it hurt. It wasn't merely a flicker of doubt—it was a force, slamming into me, dragging me back from the edge. It was as if something, or someone, refused to let me go—a jolt of electricity through my veins, a sudden, suffocating realisation: What am I doing?

Tears burned down my cheeks as I stared at the pills in my palm. My fingers loosened, and they tumbled to the floor—tiny echoes of a life I nearly threw away. My body shook, and my lungs gasped for air, as though I had just broken the surface after nearly drowning. I was still here, and something—something powerful—wanted me to stay.

I slapped myself across the face, hard, desperate to snap out of the stupor.

I had survived him. I had survived leaving. I had done the hardest part. And now, I needed to fight. Something had to change—because if it didn't, I wasn't going to make it.

The next day, I pulled myself together. My body felt heavy and my mind was fogged with exhaustion, but I forced myself to think clearly. I needed a plan. I needed to get us out of this toxic spiral. No more sinking, no more drowning in despair. I had to fight—fight to get a roof over our heads, to build something solid, something safe. That thought gave me a fragile sense of purpose. For the first time in a long time, I had something to cling to.

As Christmas crept closer with every passing day, panic set in. We had nothing—no money, no presents, no tree, no decorations. Just an empty space and the relentless weight of reality pressing down on me. In the days leading up to it, despite my determination, I felt like I was losing my mind. Anxiety ate away at me like a disease, its claws digging deeper, its whispers growing louder. Guilt sat like a stone in my chest, a constant reminder of every mistake I'd made. But I had a purpose—and it's that purpose that kept me moving.

I sat my son down one evening, my voice trembling and my hands twisting together in my lap. "I'm so sorry," I whispered, my eyes glistening with unshed tears. "I don't have any money for presents this year . . . but I promise I'll do my best for you." He looked up at me with those big, bright eyes full of something indefinable, and simply said, "It's okay, Mum."

Just three words—three little words that shattered me and stitched me back together all at once. My throat tightened, and my heart ached as I wondered how I'd ever gotten so lucky with him.

That Christmas, we made it our own. We played Monopoly, Guess Who, and Snakes and Ladders—of course, he always won. Then he wanted to play with Nerf guns, that little rascal. He shot me square in the arm, and, bloody hell, those things hurt! I pretended to be outraged, but all I could do was laugh as he let out that big, beautiful laugh—the kind that made the whole world seem a little lighter.

When the games were over, we curled up together under a cosy blanket to watch a film. His little head rested on my shoulder; his tiny hand curled around mine. At that moment, the cold, the struggle, and the uncertainty—all of it faded into insignificance. We had each other.

Looking back now, we had nothing—no money, no extravagant gifts, no fancy dinners—but in truth, we had everything that mattered: time, love, and laughter. It was, without doubt, one of the best Christmases I ever had. That little boy didn't just mend my broken heart; he gave me the strength to fight, to get up, and to push forward. For him, I would tear the world apart to build something better. I wasn't going to fail.

***

I threw myself into applying for jobs, knowing I had no choice but to keep going. It wasn't easy—nothing about this new life was. I managed to land a few jobs—cleaning, working in shops—anything that would bring in a bit of money, no matter how exhausting or soul-destroying it felt. Every single day became a relentless cycle: I'd drag myself out of bed, force a smile, and get on with work. The hours were long, the pay was barely enough, and by the time I got home, I was running on fumes. There was no time to rest; I'd make dinner, play with my son, read him a bedtime story, tuck him in with a kiss—and then, when the caravan was finally quiet, my real work would begin.

That was when I started building my business. I poured every spare minute, every last bit of energy, into it. I saved every penny I could for training because I knew I needed to build new skills if I was ever going to survive this relentless cycle. God, it was so damn hard. There were days when I felt I was running on empty, but I pushed through.

I worked in clothes that had holes in them, with trainers falling apart and soles so worn I could feel the pavement through them. I was humiliated, and embarrassed—every day, I kept my head down and avoided eye contact, hoping no one would notice. But inside, the shame burned like a fire. I hated that I had to live like this.

Yet, I carried on.

Nights were the hardest. Exhausted from work, I'd sit in front of my battered old laptop, desperately trying to teach myself how to build a website. Back then, you couldn't just use a drag-and-drop builder like today; if you didn't know how to code, you were lost. So, I studied—watching hours of tutorials, reading books, practising line after line of code until my head spun. It took months, and when I finally built something, it looked absolutely awful. I remember staring at the screen, my heart sinking. After all that effort, and all those sleepless nights, this was the best I could do. It was a disaster. But I refused to give up.

I scraped together every last bit of money I could, saved for another six months, and finally paid someone to help fix it. Piece by piece, my very first business—a dating site—came together. I'd always wanted to see people happy, to bring people together, so I thought, why not? Maybe I could create something that actually made a difference. But there was one massive problem— how on earth was I going to get it noticed? I had no money for advertising, no connections, no experience. I was stumbling in the dark, completely alone. I had a burning desire for a dating app to bring people true love and joy, but the problem was the app just didn't stand out, it was like all the others.

So I did what I always did—I learned. I immersed myself in

marketing, devouredevery free resource I could find, and trained in journalism, thinking that if I could master content creation, maybe I could generate interest. But it wasn't enough. After nearly two years of fighting and pouring my soul into something, I needed to succeed, but I had to facethe truth: it wasn't working. It was growing—but so slowly and despite having felt I'd already given it everything I had. My energy was gone. My resources were drained. I hadnothing left to give.

And so, I made the hardest decision of all: I pulled the plug.

Just like that, two years of work, sacrifice, and desperate hope were gone. I was back tosquare one.

CHAPTER SIX:

When Darkness Calls

I decided to train as a coach and therapist—specifically, a life coach, dating coach, and image consultant. Not because I had a burning desire to coach people directly, but because I wanted to help them find their soulmate. I wanted to guide them, point them towards the right therapist if needed, and help them heal so they could find real, lasting love.

What I didn't realise at the time was that in equipping myself with all the tools to helpothers, I was also unearthing everything I had buried deep inside. I threw myself into thework—head down, grafting for years—and God, was it hard. I juggled two other jobs just to keep everything afloat: cleaning and stocking shelves—the mental and physical toll wasstaggering.

I made some massive mistakes along the way—taking on clients I shouldn't have, bending over backwards to please them, trying too hard to be what they wanted instead of standing firm in my own expertise. But I kept going. Night after night, I pushed myself pastexhaustion, determined to rise above the wreckage of my past.

And then, after what felt like an eternity, something changed. I started getting good. Really good, after so many freebies. I learned to trust my instincts—when I listened, truly listened, everything just clicked. My gut never steered me wrong, and the more I honed mycraft, the more confident I became. I spent years perfecting my approach to matchmaking, refining what worked and discarding what didn't.

Out of nowhere, I began attracting high-profile clients—the elite. On the surface, it was brilliant. I was working with people who had money, influence, and seemingly endless demands. In some ways, it was easier because I could keep a professional distance. My radar was sharp and connections were made, but there was no emotional entanglement. They didn'tneed me—just what I could do for them—so I played the part, kept things running, stayed strong, and shut down everything else, because while I truly loved helping people, lettinganyone close enough to see how broken I was felt far too dangerous.

At first, it'd been exciting—a new challenge. But with that world came a whole new level of expectation. The stakes were higher, the demands more intense. These people didn't want to wait for love; they wanted it yesterday. They expected me to pluck a soulmate off a shelf as if it were as simple as ordering a takeaway.

Yes, I had clients. Yes, I could find someone who fits their physical ideal. But I wasn't in this for superficial connections. I wanted to create something real—a deep, meaningful relationship that lasted.

And yet, time and again, I was handed ridiculous lists— pages of requirements. "I want them to look like this—like Eva Longoria or a prince—elegant, radiant—untouchable."

"They need to have this job–unshakeable poise or clout." "They must have this lifestyle—glamourous."

It was laughable. These clients weren't searching for love; they were chasing perfection. And I wasn't interested. I didn't care about their ideal fantasy. What mattered was what they were willing to bring to the table.

Love isn't about a checklist. It's not about what's on the outside—it's about what's happening inside. It's about someone's depth, their purpose, the kind of love they are willing to give, and how they will treat their partner. That was the person I wanted to help. That was the kind of love I believed in.

On the outside, everything looked glamorous. My business was thriving; I was working with high-profile clients and making money. To everyone else, it seemed I had built something shining and successful. But inside, I was falling apart. I was so busy fixing everyone else's problems that I never paused to deal with my own. I had spent years helping others find love, but I had never stopped to heal myself.

I was fiercely driven to build an empire—not just to give my son the security I never had, but to help others find the kind of true love and happiness the world so often deems out of reach. Then, —ping—a message. It was from some bloke I'd been having a bit of banter with. I didn't really know him well, but, deep down, I was lonely. We got chatting. He seemed confident, even charming. Then he asked, "Can you speak?" I wasn't in the mood. "No, I'll call you tomorrow," I replied.

It's funny—people would say I had some hugely eligible bachelors chasing me, but I wasn't interested. This was work— professional boundaries were paramount. Once they became clients, there was absolutely no crossing that line; I had worked too hard to build my name and brand to let it all crumble.

However the next day, we did speak, and the conversation

flowed easily—as though we'd known each other for ages. It was nice, light, a welcome distraction from the chaos of my life. Before long, we arranged to meet. But the truth was, my head was not in the right place. I was drowning in stress, desperately trying to secure a roof over our heads. All I couldthink about was security, building something solid for me and my son. Dating wasn't really on my radar. Yet still, I went.

The moment I saw Jack, my stomach dropped. He looked nothing like his photos—atleast twenty years older, in my mind's eye. And yet, that wasn't what unsettled me most.

Something deep inside screamed, "Run."

But then, he said the words I'd been desperate to hear, "I'll help you."

And just like that, the fear was swallowed by a flicker of hope. It was as if a knight in shiningarmour had emerged, ready to take some of the weight off my shoulders. I ignored that gnawing twist in my stomach—the same one I had felt when I met John—but still, I didn't listen.

When Jack suggested another date, I hesitated. I wasn't sure whether I was feeling it.

But a friend said, "What have you got to lose?" and I was convinced once again. I shouldhave listened to myself instead of the voices around me.

Still unsure, I asked the universe for a sign. "If I'm not meant to go, let my son's school bus break down." Now, bear in mind— his bus had never broken down. Not once in all those years. I usually picked him up, or someone else did, but the bus . . . It was always on time, give or take five or ten minutes. Reliable as clockwork—never failing.

On the night I was meant to meet this guy, my phone rang. "Mum, it's me. The busbroke down."

I froze. They were just up the road, waiting for someone to come and fix it. My heartpounded so hard I could barely think. The universe had given me a crystal-clear warning—a sign I should heed. And what did I do? I ignored it. I went on the date anyway, got really pissed, and to be honest, I can't even remember much of that night.

The next day, Jack messaged me, and that's when the red flags started. At first, they were little things—a lie here, a contradiction there. But soon, the falsehoods grew bigger and bolder until alarm bells were ringing so loudly, I could hardly hear my own thoughts.

Something wasn't right. I bluntly confronted him, "You're lying!"

The phone went dead. I never heard from him again. I suspect he thought I was rich, that he could bleed me dry for money. It was frightening how quickly everything shifted. Yet,the real horror was that I still didn't trust my instincts.

So, I did what I always did—I ploughed into work. I climbed higher, attending more elite events and mingling with the right crowds. London became my second home; I was in and out of the city three or four times a week, day and night. It was exhilarating but utterly exhausting.

Then, one night at an event, I felt it—a presence. Across the room, a man was staring at me. His gaze was intense, almost predatory, as if calculating every detail of my being. I should have looked away, but I couldn't. Perhaps deep down, after everything—the loneliness, the endless fight to secure a future for me and my son—I was desperate to be wanted—desperate for love.

He walked over. "Hi, I'm Damien."

"Hi," I replied, my voice sounding smaller than I felt. We talked. He was funny, charismatic, and had that air about him that suggested he owned the room.

But before I knew it, he excused himself with a casual, "I've got to go," and just like that, he was gone.

I felt a sudden pang of disappointment—he was interesting, different, intelligent.

Then came a text message:

I'm going away for a few weeks with my kids.

Okay, have fun, I texted back. We'll speak when I get back.

Alright, I replied. And just like that, I carried on with my life, unaware of what was coming next.

Weeks passed, and I was moving through the motions, just trying to get by, until one Saturday afternoon, a message popped up on my phone:

Hi, it's Damien. Are you free to chat?

My son was at a friend's house for the night, yet I found myself standing there, stunned by the unexpected message, unsure if I was truly free. I was tired of feeling so isolated, so alone, so buried under the weight of my own thoughts.

Yeah, sure, I can talk, I replied with added gusto.

Before I knew it, we had spent five hours on the phone. Five long hours. I hadn't spoken to anyone properly in ages. It was strange—refreshing, even—that Damien could talk endlessly, his words tumbling out as if he were recounting a life lived in fast-forward. Occasionally, I'd hear him take a slurp of his drink—a sound, that oddly enough, became comforting amidst the chaos of our conversation.

"Just having a cold drink," he'd say between slurps.

At first, it felt like a welcome distraction—a light, easy conversation to momentarily dull the edges of my stress. But as he continued, I began to sense something deeper, something calculated hidden within his words. He started telling me his story—his version of events. He claimed he was a very successful businessman—huge success, he said. To this day, I'm still not sure what to believe. There was no evidence to back up his claims, but at the time, I had no reason to doubt him. He spoke so convincingly, so smoothly, that it was hard to imagine any half-truth in his narrative.

He told me about his life: his ex-wife, his kids, how he'd grown bored with his marriage despite the constant flow of money, and how, amid all that success, he'd met a model. Their affair had ignited a whirlwind of travel, endless parties, and wild escapades—as if they were living a dream. He even mentioned being on the verge of buying a private jet. He said he was living the dream.

I listened, caught between fascination and scepticism, my mind swirling with thoughts of my own precarious existence. Even as I hung on every word, a part of me whispered warnings—reminders of all the red flags I'd already ignored. And yet, I was so hungry for connection, so desperate for someone to share the burden, that I let his words wash over me. But then, the cracks started to show. Business slowed down, and the funding dried up.

Damien had invested the company's money—millions and millions—into Lehman Brothers. He had lots of meetings. Damien couldn't believe his luck; Lehman Brothers, he thought, were going to change everything. Life, he believed couldn't get better than this. At one point, Damien had nearly a billion pounds' worth of property funds. The final meeting with Lehman Brothers was supposed to change his life. He decided to go ahead with the transaction and allegedly transferred the money.

A few days later, he was in the Caribbean, waiting for a call from Lehman Brothers. But the call never came. Instead, a colleague messaged him, "I hope you haven't sent any investment money over."

Damien asked, "Why?"

"You haven't heard the news? Lehman Brothers just crashed."

Damien's world came crashing down. He had to sell his houses—one in the Bahamas and another in the UK. The funding dried up completely. He was on the verge of bankruptcy. Everything he had built was tumbling down.

I could hear the shift in his tone—there was a heaviness, a strain that hadn't been there before. The pressure was mounting—and it weighed on him like a physical force.

Damien began to tell me about his girlfriend and how she'd turned toxic—always drinking, always doing drugs. The same woman he'd once adored had become a burden, a constant drain on his already fragile spirit. And when they had their first child, a little boy, things had seemed fine for a while. But then . . . the money ran out. That's when the real damage happened. As soon as the funds dried up, she left him. Just like that. When the money was gone, so was the façade she had maintained. She wasn't interested in him any more—she cared only about the lifestyle he could provide. He said she had spent every day shopping, keeping up appearances. And when the money wasn't there, she couldn't keep theact up.

She left him, and he told me with a raw, piercing pain in his voice how not only hadshe stopped him from seeing his boy, but she'd also stopped him from seeing his little girl.

The sense of loss in his tone was unbearable. The bitterness he felt at being pushed out of his kids' lives, unable to see them or make things right—it all shattered something inside me. My heart cracked a little at that moment.

As the weeks slipped by, we kept talking. He'd message me, and I'd reply until I found myself increasingly drawn to his story. There was a connection—a shared sense of loss and desperation that resonated deep within me, as though we had both lost everything. I could feel his pain like it was my own, and that massive, raw connection filled me with both empathy and pity. I started to believe that perhaps, in our shared misery, we could find solacetogether.

Damien began coming over more regularly, and with that, my drinking habit returned—again and again. On weekends, when I didn't have my son with me, I'd end up getting drunk with him. The alcohol flowed freely, and every clink of his glass and slurped sip were reminders of the red flags I should have seen. There were signs, subtle at first—a liehere, an inconsistency there—but I ignored them. I let him pull me in deeper, seduced by the idea that I was the one person who could help him, that I could somehow mend the broken pieces of his life.

One night, after another of those long, exhausting phone calls, he broke down. "I can't cope," he admitted, his voice cracking. "I can't lose my kids, and my business is falling apart. It's all slipping away." His words hung in the air, heavy and desperate. At that moment, my heart ached for him. I was already so emotionally invested—I felt his pain, his despair as if it were my own. I thought, with every fibre of my being, that I understood him. I had lost so much too, and understood firsthand how painful losing everything could be.

"I promise you," I said, voice trembling with determination and sorrow, "I'll help you.

I'll help you get your kids back. We'll build you up again. I'll help you get your business back on track." I wanted to believe that I could be his saviour, the person who would rescuehim from this downward spiral. I thought that by giving him hope, I could heal the wounds that ran so deep in both of us.

I wanted to be the one who made a difference, the one who could pull him from thebrink. We had more than a connection— rather a profound bond forged in our shared lossesand pain. I felt his struggle as if it were my own, and my pity for him mingled with a desperate desire to fix what was broken. Yet looking back, I realise I was only feeding his need to be rescued. While he had me in his grip, I was too blinded by low self-esteem and loneliness to see it.

His slurping and slurring while drinking became more frequent, more insistent—a constant background noise that should have signalled danger. Each time I heard that familiar sound, I should've known better. I should have stopped listening, should have drawn a line. But I didn't. I wanted to believe that I was the one person who could help him, that I could make everything right again. Instead, I was sinking further into his story, into the drama and the pain that had become our shared reality.

Yet, even as I reached out to help him, I couldn't shake the nagging voice inside me—a voice that warned me of the danger of losing myself completely in someone else'smisery. I knew that every red flag, every inconsistency in his story, was a sign that I was

spiralling into the same old trap. But I was too far in, too emotionally invested, to pull backnow.

I continued to let his pain, his failures, and his self-destruction become intertwined with my own life. And with each passing day, our connection grew—intense, maddening, andall-consuming. I felt as if his losses were my own, and our shared sense of vulnerability bound us together in a way that was as intoxicating as it was dangerous.

CHAPTER SEVEN:

Hanging by a Thread

The Final Betrayal

I worked tirelessly for years, often doing free work just to build my name. Then came a life-changing call—a major company from the USA, after scouring the globe for matchmakers, reached out. Out of hundreds interviewed, they had narrowed it down to three.

I was one of them. The possibility of having my own TV show—my own platform—was suddenly within reach. This could be the security I'd been fighting for. So, I threw myself into the process: weeks of interviews, endless preparation, late nights and early mornings, all blending into one feverish drive. Eventually, it was down to two candidates—me and one other— and they told me they loved me. It felt so close, so tantalisingly nearby.

Meanwhile, at home, things were unravelling. Damien—the man I had supported through his darkest hours—had finally regained custody of his kids. I had stood by him, helped build his business from scratch, and things had seemed to be looking up for him, if only for moments at a time. I took care of his children, picked them up and entertained them, all while still juggling my own work and caring for my son. My son, now a preteen, valued his independence yet still clung to our moments together. I was proud of the kind, big-heartedboy he was becoming.

When Damien was good, he was really good. Those moments were like lifelines—abreath of fresh air after drowning in chaos. He would teach me about business, sharing his knowledge as if it were something precious that could lift me out of the endless mire I was stuck in. He'd patiently help my son, make him laugh, play, with him and show him what itmeant to be cared for. In those moments, everything clicked, and I saw what could be—a future built on partnership and genuine connection, a life we could construct together. It was more than just good; it was exhilarating. For those fleeting moments, all felt real. I had foundsomeone who understood my pain, someone who had lost everything just as I had, and whosesuffering mirrored my own. I felt a massive connection and a deep, abiding pity for him that resonated with my very soul.

But Damien was a volatile presence. When he was good, he was really good. But when he wasn't . . . It was a whole different story. His drinking began to spiral out of control.

I would watch him deteriorate—by mid-afternoon most days, he'd be so drunk he'd pass out. I tried everything: taking him to AA meetings, forcing therapy sessions, even surprising him with scheduled counselling, hoping something would finally stick. But nothing changed. He kept drinking, and I kept covering for him, hiding it from his children, desperately maintaining the façade of normality.

As the weeks passed, the call from the USA grew quieter— no news, only almost deafening silence. Then finally, an email arrived. I hadn't gotten the part. My heart shattered. I had pinned my security on this opportunity. I cried. I grieved the loss of that dream.

But then, the next day, something inside me snapped. Sod it, I thought. If they won't give me a show, I'll create my own. Fuelled by determination and raw desperation, I conceived a brand-new TV concept—a vision entirely my own. I was proud of it. I reached out to a friend in the industry, who loved the idea and passed it along to a contact with 25 years of experience in television. Within days, I found myself on a Zoom call, nerves buzzing, yet clinging to hope. Little did I know who I was speaking to. The person on the other end was friendly and professional, asking insightful questions. At the end of the call, they said, "We love it. We'd like to be executive producers."

Afterward, I did my research and nearly collapsed. One of the women involved was one of the biggest names on TV, with shows she had created becoming household staples. And she had chosen me. Thank God I hadn't known her identity before the call—I would have been a stammering mess, no different than Chandler from Friends would be when meeting a celebrity.

The message I want to leave you with is this: if something doesn't work out, try another way. There's always another way. Had I gotten the original show in the USA, I would have owned nothing. But this—this show, this concept—I owned a piece of it, and that made all the difference.

I was exhilarated. One half of my life was finally falling into place; my career was taking off in ways I had only dared to dream of. Yet the other half—the part that involved my turbulent relationship with Damien—was spiralling out of control. I was mentally exhausted, constantly holding him up, supporting him, and making excuses for his behaviour.

I got his children back, and during the summer holidays, I entertained them, even though it was exhausting being a single parent with Damien's destructive habits. He would drink by mid-afternoon until he was as useful as a chocolate teapot.

It felt as if he were a weight around my neck, slowly pulling me under. Covering for a grown man—a 50-plus-year-old man, no less—was draining the very life from me. He should have known better. Why wasn't he owning his actions and taking responsibility? He had everything he wanted, yet he squandered it all. I couldn't understand. All I could do was focus on my career because, if I was being honest, what else could I do for Damien?

So, I worked hard. Meetings, calls, endless hustling. Eventually, I had a breakthrough—a reworked TV concept. With help from a TV executive, we developed the idea, shot a pilot, and prepared to pitch it. For those who don't know, a pilot is a small test version of a show used to sell the concept to networks. It was a turning point, a glimmer of hope after so many years of struggle.

The night before a critical day of filming, I was a bundle of nerves. Damien had insisted on coming along, promising he wouldn't drink—a promise I never truly trusted. How could I? Most days, he was drunk. Why would this time be any different? To avoid being late for the early shoot in London, I drove up the night before, staying alone so I could focus. My son was with friends and safe. The dog was cared for. For once, I had nothing else to worry about.

But the truth was, life was akin to living with a reckless, unpredictable child. And the moment I really stepped back, I saw it all so clearly—I had been walking on constant eggshells around him, suffocating under the weight of my own vigilance. Yet, I couldn't think about any of that. Not then. That day, I had to focus on the show.

When filming began, I was on edge, sweating and checking every time the door opened, hoping Damien would keep his promise. And then, he walked in. My heart raced—was he sober? Was he even in a straight line? I was so preoccupied with managing his every move that I wasn't fully present for the moment I'd worked so hard for. As it turned out, he was sober, but it was only in hindsight that I was able to grasp how utterly exhausting it all had been—constantly juggling, balancing, and keeping the peace while planning five steps ahead to prevent disaster. Did I really want to live like this? It was soul-destroying.

I know some of you reading this will understand. Watching someone with so much talent, so much potential, just waste it all—it's heartbreaking. I had spent years managing everything, eliminating every potential negative, even controlling who came to the door to hide the chaos. Daily, after 2 or 3 p.m., I had to be extra vigilant, ensuring my son was safe and that he'd be protected from the worst of it all. But inside, I felt like a terrible mother. Had I subjected him to all of this? Again? All I had ever wanted was a loving, stable home. Why was that so impossible? The guilt gnawed at me every day.

And then, I began to work on something else—a new chapter of my life that could perhaps heal the wounds in the face of all the chaos. I still felt connected to Damien in a way that terrified and comforted me all at once. That overwhelming connection—raw, intense, and filled with pity—pulled me in deeper, even while trying to build my own empire.

But I couldn't stop. I was in too deep. And this TV show? It was our security. I owned nothing—no home, no stability. The show's success was critical, especially since Damien wasn't bringing in money—he was merely borrowing from his poor mother. She was so lovely and kind, and I couldn't help but feel for her. She had been through this before, holding him up as I was now as if we were both raising a grown child together. But why?

Why couldn't he take responsibility? He had every chance—therapy and support groups. I even called AA for guidance. They assured me I was doing the right thing, and that I should keep encouraging him. But he wouldn't go. I offered to sit with him, to support him in any way—waiting inside, or outside if that was what he needed. He just . . . wouldn't.

The TV show wrapped, and then it became a waiting game. Physically and emotionally, I was drained. Yet, amid the despair, there was a glimmer of hope. A few months later, we got the call. The biggest distributor in the world wanted the show—set to be broadcast across 27 countries, including Spain, Germany, the USA, India, and Canada. This was it. Maybe, finally, I could afford to put Damien in rehab. Maybe that would save him because I was at my wit's end.

Then, an executive wanted to meet in London to discuss the next steps. Years and years of work, nearly a decade of sacrifice, hustling in a caravan, scraping by on almost nothing—and now, an opportune meeting that could change everything.

The executive arranged for us to meet at a private members' club where he often presented. Damien overheard the call and insisted on coming. I told him no—I begged him to stay home. But he swore on his life he wouldn't drink, knowing how much this meant. And once again, I foolishly believed him.

***

The day came. I had my meetings and had sorted care for my son and the dog—everything was meticulously planned, like preparing for a new baby. I arrived ten minutes early, calm and ready. The executive and I sat down, and he ordered a bottle of wine. I barely touched my glass, taking just a sip or two. But then—Damien walked in.

My body went cold. I held my breath as my heart pounded, realising instantly he was drunk. His stagger, his dishevelled expression—it was all too obvious. And I still had nearly an hour left in this crucial meeting. In a matter of minutes, he grabbed the wine and downed most of it, his voice rising into a cascade of profanities. I wanted nothing more than to sink through the floor. The executive was visibly humiliated, and we had to physically remove

Damien—practically dragging and carrying him out—until a taxi finally stopped. I got him back to the station, fuming inside. How could he do this? Why had I believed him again?

The next morning, I woke early with a fierce determination. Enough was enough. I told him we needed to talk. I had done everything—helped him rebuild his life, reconnect with his kids, supported his failing business—but I couldn't do it any longer. I was shattered.

Then came the same old script:

"I'm sorry. I'll never drink again. I promise."

I couldn't stand it. I needed space. I told him I was going to Sainsbury's for groceries, just to get some air. Hours passed. I paced the aisles, still seething with anger and numb with hurt. And then, as I loaded the shopping into the car, my phone buzzed with a missed call and a text message from one of the TV executives:

Lisa, what is going on?

Damien had emailed everyone in our group—the TV directors, the executives, the top decision-makers who had been clamouring for our show. When I saw it, my stomach churned. I felt physically sick and couldn't bring myself to open it at first. I had only been away for a few hours—what could he have done in such a short time?

Finally, with bated breath and shaking hands, I opened the message. My heart sank.

This was my one chance for security, for a better life—and it felt as though he had obliterated it in one fell swoop. His email was calculated, articulate, and scathing. The grammar was flawless, the tone as professional as it was venomous—it wasn't the incoherent rambling of someone drunk; it was a premeditated, cutting attack from someone who knew exactly how to wound me.

He accused me of being incompetent and worthless at my job. I couldn't believe it. This man, who claimed to love me—the man I had stood by through his darkest moments, who I had tried so desperately to help—was now undermining me completely. After everything I had done—supporting him through his drinking, cleaning up his messes, holding him together when he fell apart—this was how he repaid me?

I broke down in tears, sobbing in the car park, feeling utterly betrayed. All I had ever wanted was for the show to succeed, to give us both financial stability, a safe home for the kids, and maybe even a holiday free from the constant stress. And in one calculated act, he had shattered that hope. The betrayal cut deeper than anything else, leaving me to question everything—had he ever truly loved me, or had he simply loved the support I provided? I had never experienced anything like this before. Living with an addict is soul-destroying, and I was beyond my breaking point. There's only so much a person can take.

I finally called the TV director and told him the truth—

Damien was an alcoholic. He said he had suspected as much after overhearing some of our calls and recognising the signs. "Lisa, this isn't going to work," he said gently. I knew he was right.

I sat in my car for what seemed like hours, numb as if I had just lost years of my life. Years of hard work, building, planning—all of it, gone. But I had to think of my son. I had to think of myself. I couldn't do this anymore.

want you to imagine standing in your kitchen—the kettle on the counter, the warmth of the oven, the quiet hum of the fridge. You open it to find butter, cheese, milk—those little comforts you never think twice about. You walk through your home, the floor beneath your feet grounding you, the familiar weight of your bed and the neatly hung clothes in your wardrobe reassuring you. Now, imagine knowing that by tomorrow, all of it will be gone. No kettle. No fridge. No carpet beneath your feet. No bed to sink into. No wardrobe filled with your clothes. That feeling of security ripped away in an instant.

I felt sick. This was the second time I had to walk away from everything. The first time with John had been hard enough.

But it was all for my son. I was his mother, his protector. And yet, I was uprooting him once again, forcing him into uncertainty, into nothingness. The weight of that reality crushed me. What kind of mother does this to her child?

When I got home, I told Damien I was leaving for a week. "Stay here as long as you need to sort yourself out," I said. Then, deeply ashamed and embarrassed, I called my mum. I hated asking for help, but I was broken. I only told her part of the story—I couldn't bear to share the full extent of the humiliation I felt. I just wanted to hide under the covers and disappear. I packed a few things, hoping and praying that maybe this would be the wake-upcall he desperately needed to turn his life around.

I had survived him. I had survived leaving. I had done the hardest part—or so I thought. Now, I had to fight. I had to change my life—because if I didn't, I wouldn't make it.

CHAPTER EIGHT:

The Edge of Darkness

I stayed with my parents, and although I was in a fragile state, I felt a fleeting sense of relief—no more babysitting, no more constantly being five steps ahead to cover forDamien. Deep down, though, I knew his property business would collapse without me screening his calls. For one brief moment, I believed I might finally be safe. Then themessages started:

Call me?

Where are you?

The messages and calls flooded in—relentless, overwhelming. Soon came emails and even posts on the business's social media, where he hurled unspeakable names (often even misspelt) in a desperate bid to humiliate me. His harassment escalated: 20, 30, sometimes 60calls a day, countless texts accusing me of stealing his TV, taking his phone, and sending bizarre lies to my clients—with his mother cc'd for added shame.

Even though his poor mother tried to explain that someone had found his phone on the high street and returned it to the police, Damien only grew louder and crueller. "You're aslag," he wrote. All I had ever done was love him, support him, and clean up his literal and emotional messes. So why was he so unkind?

Granted, I know he grew up poor and bullied, and though I saw his potential, he never tried—and that made me angry.

The barrage continued for weeks, and then the weeks turned into months. He began turning up at my mum's house. The first time, my dad was there and firmly told Damien to leave, claiming he was drunk. After that, the texts worsened, emails filled with slurs and absurd accusations like "Lisa is a druggy." The only "drug" I'd taken was a paracetamol—a feeble comparison to his delusions. His lies were absurd, yet his behaviour—terrifying.

I recalled how he used to warn me about his ex, painting her as unstable. But when I finally met her, she was calm, kind, polite—just a woman who wore sunglasses in the winter. I never questioned it then, but now I understood why she left him.

Ignoring him only seemed to fuel his madness. It was as if he were having entire conversations with himself, sending messages as though I'd replied. I was exhausted, broke, and mentally shattered. Bills piled up with no income from the TV show, and soon creditors began calling, demanding payments I simply couldn't manage. My body and mind were breaking down. I just couldn't work, I didn't have the mental capacity, and it brought me to the edge.

Then the landlord rang. "You need to do something, Lisa," he said, exasperation lacing his tone. "Damien is bringing strangers back, neighbours are complaining, cider cans are everywhere—he's out of control."

Then he said someone found him on the lawn, hugging a tree, only to later discover him passed out nearby.

In desperation, I reached out to his family. "He's scaring me. Please help." "We know," they admitted wearily. "He's done this before."

Of course, he had—they'd been babysitting him long before I ever had to step in. I had merely been giving them a break. They advised me to call the police if things worsened. I couldn't help but wonder why I was still protecting him; it all felt utterly stupid.

For one day, there was blissful silence. I thought he'd finally come to his senses. But the next day, the calls resumed, even worse than before. Now he was accusing me of seeing other men—twisting reality so completely I felt as if I were losing my mind. I hadn't even considered another relationship; I was so broken, so terrified of men now, after the devastation left by those I'd once trusted.

Damien's threats grew darker. "I'm going to destroy you," he snarled. He even called my accountant—a kind, hardworking man—and harassed him until the fear in his voice was unmistakable. That was when I'd realised, I was well past the breaking point.

I begged him to stop. I told him he could still see the kids, that I'd still drive him two hours, both ways, to pick them up, just so he wouldn't lose them—but I could never be with him again. I hoped that maybe, just maybe, giving him some dignity might help him rebuild. But of course, it didn't. Then came the final blow: Damien claimed he had a friend who was going to "shut down my business and take me out."

That was it. Something inside me cracked in a way I'd never felt before. My body felt like it had turned to glass—already shattered, sharp and splintered into too many pieces to count. I was teetering on the edge of a nervous breakdown. Exhausted. Terrified. Trembling from the inside out.

This nearly broke me.

All those years—*years*—of agony, of building something from absolutely nothing, and of holding it together when everything around me was falling apart. Working two, sometimes three jobs. Living in a freezing caravan with no toilet. Skipping meals just to keep the lights on. Sacrificing holidays, new clothes, any scrap of comfort—because I believed in something. I poured every drop of myself into that business. Into that dream. And now? It felt as though none of it mattered. Like he could rip it all away in a single breath.

I wasn't just tired. I was beyond burned out. I felt hollow— like a version of me had died somewhere along the way, and no one had noticed. I smiled on the outside, sure. I was strong for everyone else. But inside, I was barely breathing. What little hope I had left flickered—faint and fragile. I felt invisible in my own life—stripped down to the bare mechanics of survival.

It wasn't just my business on the line. It was me. How could he do this? How could someone who once claimed to love me— who I'd stood by through in his darkest moments—watch me bleed for something and then rip it from my hands without a second thought? It wasn't just my business—it was my survival, my future, and the proof that I wasn't the failure people once believed I was. The betrayal burned through me. The injustice made me want to scream, yet I had no fight left. I'd been brought to my knees, at the thought of losing the one thing I'd built from ashes.

The threats were getting worse, alongside the insults: "Fat slag" and "Fat girls are all the same," and "You are one."

Then came the threats to kill me.

I couldn't be brave any longer. I called the police, and they told me to keep records—write everything down. But the situation only escalated. Damien said he was coming to my house to kill me, and I couldn't stop shaking.

That afternoon, while my son was at his friend's house, my mum and I sat on the sofa, talking and crying as we tried to make sense of it all. Out of the corner of my eye, I saw him—creeping around the back of the house. I got up and never ran so fast, I bolted for the door, heart pounding, and managed to lock it just as he grabbed the handle. He pounded on the door, his shouts echoing through the house. I could barely speak or think.

Hiding in the bedroom with my mum, I called the police again while he raged outside banging on the doors and windows that had been double-checked and locked every day since my arrival. Every morning, I checked and rechecked like a ritual. But that day, I'd missed locking the main door.

He was screaming, unhinged, as he pounded on the house. My mum and I sat in silence, crouched on the bedroom floor, hearts pounding in our throats, barely able to breathe. The air was thick with fear—hot, suffocating, charged with a kind of danger you can feel in your bones.

Then he turned to my car. The alarm exploded into the stillness of the day, and the piercing noise shot straight through me. My mum trembled beside me. I was frozen, with my fingers clenched so tightly around the phone that my hand went numb. We didn't move.

Didn't speak. Just listened—helpless, terrified—as the man I once loved tried to destroy everything within reach.

I knew—deep down in my gut—that if he managed to get in,

something terrible would happen. He was beyond reason. There was no trace of the man I had known. Just a storm of rage and something cold behind his eyes.

When the blue lights finally pulled into the drive, I broke. The flood of emotion was tortuous—relief, humiliation, panic, gratitude—all tangled in my chest, tightening like a fist.

I was in deep shock. My whole body felt numb and electric at the same time. Like I was watching it all happen from somewhere far away.

I had reached a level of exhaustion I didn't know existed. The kind that seeps into your soul. That day nearly broke me for good. I wasn't just scared—I was cracked wide open.

Every part of me was frayed, scattered, like broken glass on a floor no one had bothered to sweep up.

Something inside me had died in those hours. Some last piece of trust, or hope, or innocence—I don't even know what to call it. But whatever it was, it was gone.

***

Damien's family soon came to collect his belongings. I knew he'd been there, and although he was miles away now, stepping inside the apartment filled me with dread. My hands shook as I reached for the door handle, my breath shallow. I hesitated before pushing the door open, bracing myself.

Inside, a wave of fear washed over me. The house felt different—darker, heavier, as though the walls were still clinging to the chaos that had unfolded. The air was thick and suffocating, echoing with memories of slammed doors, bitter arguments, and the venom in his voice.

Then I was hit by the stench.

Faeces were smeared on the sofa, cupboards were cluttered with empty cans and vomit, and every room reeked with filth. It resembled a squat: a shelter for the broken, and in it, a constant reminder of everything that had gone wrong. With each step, memories flooded back: the living room where I sat too afraid to speak, the hallway where I stood frozen as his rage filled the air, and in the kitchen where I once made meals in silence, treading on eggshells.

Then I saw it—complete wreckage. His presence had been erased, but not without destruction. With cupboards left open, drawers emptied in disarray, and possessions tossed about as if they meant nothing, the apartment had been gutted, stripped away of any sense of safety it once had.

I swallowed hard and forced myself to move, room by room. I walked through the ruins, haunted by the ghosts of what once was, feeling both humiliated and broken, but I knew one thing for certain—I was never going back.

Damien was gone. It'd felt like a cloud lifted yet fear still gripped me. It took a week to clean the place: we had to rip up and replace the carpets, and burn almost everything—clothes, furniture, anything soiled in the chaos that he'd left behind. The place mimicked a disaster zone, and I felt sick to my stomach, wondering how my life had come to this.

My mum and I scrubbed for days, scouring every inch until the house finally smelled normal again. It looked clean, almost as if nothing had happened, but the scars lingered deep within me. I handed my notice to the landlord. Then after returning the keys with an apology, I left. Yet, even with my son by my side, I was too scared to be outside and constantly glanced over my shoulder, terrified. It'd taken months for me to feel safe enough to go grocery shopping alone.

The emails continued, despite blocking him. The police assured me they had all the evidence they needed—they'd seized his phone, downloaded everything, and issued an injunction. The case was now in the hands of the Crown Prosecution Service (CPS), yet he kept emailing, blatantly violating the order.

Desperate for peace, I contacted the police again. PC Brown, my hero, promised he'd ensure Damien never contacted me again. "You will need to go to court," he said gently but firmly.

Meanwhile, debt collectors kept calling. The financial strain was agonizing—I was barely holding it together, teetering on the edge of complete collapse. And then, as if it couldn't get worse, Christmas loomed. Another Christmas with no money, no presents, and no hope. Exhausted and broken, I received a call from the car company: they were going to repossess my car. I resignedly drove it to the meeting point and handed over the keys, feeling utterly defeated. No job. No car. No home. No future.

And Damien? He pleaded not guilty. Despite the mountain of evidence I had painstakingly gathered—every threatening message, every email—he maintained his innocence. One of the TV executives he'd targeted was even prepared to testify, having been harassed and threatened by him too. A respected professional with over 30 years of unblemished service had become another victim of Damien's venom. Yet, even with all this proof, I still felt crushed.

Christmas came and went in a blur of forced smiles and half-hearted celebrations. I did my best for my son, concealing the pain behind feigned normality. As he grew older and began spending more time with friends, he later confided that some of his most cherished memories were our quiet, precious cuddles. Without his constant companionship, my dog

Holly became my lifeline during bleak days. She pulled me from bed each morning for our walks and curled up beside me when I cried myself to sleep. Holly was my steady source of comfort—a living miracle that kept me tethered to hope.

But then, on the 29th of December, my world unexpectedly shattered.

***

That morning began as any other, except for the ominous sky, but I still took Holly for herusual walk; her tail wagging with boundless energy as she playfully chewed on twigs, her eyes alight with life. When we returned, she ate her breakfast with a contented enthusiasm that made me believe, even if just for a moment, that peace was possible. I watched her rest, a rare glimmer of serenity in my otherwise storm-tossed heart. But an hour later, everything changed.

Without warning, Holly began running frantically, her joy replaced by panic. In an instant, she collapsed. I watched in horror as her back legs curled unnaturally, shrivelling as though she were melting—like the Wicked Witch in *The Wizard of Oz*. I froze, my mind unable to process the unfolding nightmare. I desperately hoped she'd get up, that this was just a fleeting moment of distress, but she could not. The pain etched in her eyes was unmistakable.

I managed to lift her into my mum's car, every second drenched in anguish. Outside, the storm raged—rain lashing the windows, the world reduced to a blur as the satnav misdirected me. I sobbed uncontrollably, every twist of the road echoing the turmoil in my heart. After what felt like an eternity, I finally reached the vets and they whisked her away immediately, their eyes mirroring my despair.

"We'll keep her overnight," they said softly. I returned home, my heart shattered intoirreparable fragments.

The next morning, I sat by the phone, desperate for any word. By 9:30 a.m. there'd still been only silence. My heart pounded as I called them.

"It's not looking good," they admitted. "Another vet is going to assess her, and we'll call you later." The afternoon passed in agonising limbo.

Later, I was told, "We need to keep her for a couple more nights. We're doingeverything we can."

I didn't know how I was going to afford vet bills, but nothing mattered—I'd doanything to save Holly, but then three days later, the vet's call pierced my fragile hope.

"Her spinal cord has been snapped," they said gently. "Her bladder is damaged. She will never walk again, nor will she be able to relieve herself without constant infections. It would be cruel to keep her alive."

I begged, "What about wheels? A wee bag? I'll take care of her!""She would be in constant pain. It's time to let her go."

They say that the only thing a pet asks for when they leave is that you be there. So, my son and I stayed with her as she slipped away, our hands cradling her frail body. I was in pieces; my son's uncontrollable sobbing only deepened the wound. The drive home was a blurred haze of grief. We took her with us, wrapping her in her favourite blanket along with her cherished toys and treats. The next day, we buried her. It was the most heart-wrenching moment of my life—losing Holly ripped my heart apart. She had been my steadfast anchor in the storm, the miracle that held me together.

I collapsed into bed and remained there for days, numb and motionless. My son sought refuge at his girlfriend's house, too broken to face the emptiness of home. I was utterly spent— emotionally, mentally, physically. And then, as if the universe wasn't done with me, Damien messaged again with vile words:

Fat slag Fat girl

You are all the same—You are one

His disgust cut deeper than any physical wound. It was too much. I snapped completely.

I lay in bed, staring at the ceiling as the weight of the world bore down on me. The silence was deafening, suffocating in its stillness. I whispered to the universe, "I'm sorry. I can't do this anymore. I'm done." My shattered and battered mind teetered on the brink. I had fought so hard for so long, clinging desperately to the hope that things might get better, that I could somehow mend my broken self. But at that moment, the exhaustion, the constant battle, the overwhelming pain—it all became unbearable.

Despair led me to contemplate ending it all once more. Could I really sink any lower? My thoughts swirled like a violent storm, each one crashing into the next. Every bone in my body ached with a weariness no sleep could remedy, and my chest felt as if it were caving in. The idea of escaping the endless pain, of finally silencing the constant ache in my heart, beckoned like a forbidden escape. I just wanted to go to sleep and never wake up again.

I was utterly drained—a mere shell of the person I once was, devastated by years of physical torment and relentless battles within my own mind. An overwhelming wave of embarrassment and humiliation crashed over me, suffocating me with questions: Why was I so stupid? Why did I keep letting people hurt me? What was wrong with me? All I had ever wanted was love—to be seen, to be heard, to feel safe and cherished. Was that truly too muchto ask?

I moved to the cupboard, my hands shaking uncontrollably, the world around me blurring as I teetered on the edge of oblivion. Just as I was about to surrender and take my life, the power went out. The entire house plunged into darkness.

I couldn't see anything. The familiar comfort of my home dissolved into oppressiveshadows, the darkness swallowing every last bit of hope. It was terrifying—an all-encompassing void that pressed in on me, making it hard to breathe. But somehow, in that disorienting blackness, something shifted inside me. It wasn't an immediate relief, nor was it a sudden burst of happiness, but a quiet stirring—a fragile, almost imperceptible glimmer of hope. It was as if the universe had heard my silent plea and was now offering me a sign that maybe . . . just maybe, I wasn't meant to give up yet.

After what seemed like an eternity, the power returned. I slowly got to my feet, my body trembling and unsteady, as if learning to walk again. I reached for a glass of water, myhands still shaking, uncertain if I was awake or trapped in a dream. I returned to bed, but everything felt different. The numbness persisted; the tears were heavy in my chest like a weight I could scarcely bear. For days, I sat in quiet despair, the grief a thick fog that refusedto lift. The boundaries between days blurred, and I wondered if I would ever feel whole again.

But somehow, against all odds, I survived. The world didn't

stop turning, and despite the mess of it all, I managed to take one tentative step forward. It wasn't easy, and it wasn't immediate, but I survived—and in that fragile survival, there was a spark of hope that maybe, just maybe, there was something on the other side of the storm worth fighting for.

CHAPTER NINE:

Losing Holly; Finding Faith

Holly's passing shattered me. It broke something deep inside—a part of me that I wasn't sure could ever be repaired. It took nearly a week before I could even step outside again, forcing myself to walk, to eat properly. Every day mirrored trudging through a fog of despair, the simplest acts of living transformed into monumental challenges. I felt utterly hollow, as though a part of me had died alongside her. The weight of everything— years of pain, loss, and overwhelming exhaustion—crashed down on me all at once, leaving me gasping for breath under its relentless pressure. Yet, more than anything, I couldn't stop thinking about Holly. Was she okay? Was she at peace, free from the pain of this cruel world? The thought of her suffering tormented me more than any physical ache ever could.

One dismal afternoon, I forced myself out for a walk. I didn't want to see anyone or exchange a single word; I just needed to be alone with my thoughts. I wandered aimlessly into the woods, my feet dragging over the cold, damp earth as though each step were a battle against my own grief. The trees around me, silent and indifferent, stood as mute witnesses to my despair. Amid that profound solitude, I stopped, closed my eyes, and let my heart speak its truth. Surrounded only by the whisper of the wind and the rustling of leaves, I raised my voice—a trembling, desperate murmur barely louder than a whisper.

"Universe, please . . . let me know Holly is okay. I just need to know she's not in pain.

I can't bear the thought of her suffering. Please, give me a sign. And I swear I'll do my best to move forward. Just . . . please, please, God, help me—I just can't carry on. Give me a sign,please, and I promise I will do my best to carry on."

I waited, my eyes scanning the horizon, my ears straining for any sign of an answer.

But nothing happened. No sudden gust of wind to caress my tear-stained cheeks, no flickering light breaking through the grey of my despair—just the oppressive silence of a universe that seemed deaf to my plea. I exhaled shakily, wiped my face with the back of my hand, and turned back towards home, half-convinced that I was being utterly ridiculous.

Days passed in a blur of numb routine. I buried that desperate plea deep within my thoughts, too ashamed to tell anyone—family or friends—for fear they would label me mad or weak. It was a secret sorrow, one I carried like a hidden scar.

Then, one seemingly ordinary day, I found myself stepping outside again for yet another walk—a feeble attempt to pull myself together, to grasp at the frayed ends of my shattered life. I returned home, mechanically grabbed something to eat, and drifted towards the wall near the kitchen. And then, my breath caught in my throat.

I froze.

There, emblazoned on the wall as though by some impossible force, was a sign. My heart pounded so fiercely I thought it might shatter my ribcage. I hadn't expected anything; I hadn't even really recalled my desperate plea in such vivid detail.

But there it was—a clear, undeniable message that felt both impossible and miraculous.

I stood transfixed, my mind awash with questions and wonder. To this day, I still can't explain it. It was a miracle. An absolute, bewildering miracle. The image was unmistakable—a print of Holly, rendered not by paint or pencil, but as if by some divine imprint. My family would never have dared to create something so personal and surreal. It was as if God himself had reached out, offering me solace in the form of that small, yet profoundly significant, image. It felt as though, in that singular moment, I was being reminded that I was not utterly alone—that even in my darkest hour, there was a glimmer of care watching over me.

After everything—the endless barrage of pain, the relentless descent into despair, and hitting rock bottom yet again—I realised, quite slowly, that I was still here. Despite everything, I was still breathing. And that, however faintly, had to mean something. Perhaps I was meant for more. Perhaps all this suffering, all these battles I'd fought, were somehow leading me to a destiny beyond the relentless sorrow.

I had no clue what that destiny was, no roadmap to follow amidst the chaos of my life.

But one thing was clear: I couldn't remain stuck in a bottomless pit. Tired, exhausted, and feeling more broken than I ever thought possible, I knew I had to push through, however littleprogress I might make at a time. So, I began again.

I got up.

One morning, out of the blue, I felt a strange, undeniable pull—a calling deep insideme that I couldn't ignore. It was as if a gentle voice, buried beneath layers of pain and resignation, was urging me to seek out something new, something healing. That pull led me,against all my instincts, to a church.

Now, if you'd known me back then, you'd probably laugh at the idea. Church? Me? Ina million years I wouldn't have thought to seek solace within such sacred walls. I wasn't religious. I didn't pray. The rituals and traditions of church were as foreign to me as a language I'd never learned. But something inside me insisted that I needed to go, that perhaps, amidst the hymns and quiet prayers, I might find a fragment of hope.

Still, I had no idea what I was doing. Wasn't attending church just on Sundays? Did they even hold services on weekdays? And what on earth did people wear to church? The thought of rummaging through my wardrobe for a flowery dress and a bonnet made me laughnervously, filling me with anxiety. I was genuinely apprehensive about stepping into a world I'd never been part of before.

Like any modern, somewhat clueless soul, I turned to Google. I spent hours scouringthe internet—searching for advice on what to wear, what to say, and even whether I'd be expected to sing along (God forbid, I thought, imagining myself faltering through a hymn). Iread about church etiquette, tried to understand the unwritten rules, and even looked up tips on how not to feel completely out of place. The last thing I wanted was to walk in and immediately feel like an imposter in someone else's sanctuary.

Despite my nerves and the uncertainty swirling in my mind, I summoned the courage to go. I stepped out of the familiar darkness of my home, leaving behind the echoes of my grief, and ventured towards this new beginning—an uncertain journey towards healing, however small that hope might be.

And so, with a heavy heart and trembling hands, I stepped into a new chapter of my life, raw and scarred by loss, yet clinging to that miraculous sign on the wall. I was still here, still fighting, and in the midst of the chaos, I held on to the belief that perhaps, just perhaps, there was something greater waiting for me on the other side of this storm.

The journey was far from over, and the path ahead remained shrouded in uncertainty, but for that moment, I stood on the threshold of the church car park and took a tentative step. I allowed myself to believe that even in the darkest nights, a new dawn was possible.

I remember standing outside that church door for the first time, my heart hammering against my ribs seemingly wanting to escape the despair that had become my constant companion. It felt as though I didn't belong—like I was intruding on something reserved for

people unburdened by a dark past, weighed down by so much pain that it rendered them almost immobile. Yet, despite every fibre of my being urging me to flee, I stepped inside.

No sooner had I crossed the threshold than the vicar spotted me. He offered a warm, inviting smile and greeted me kindly. I barely returned his smile—only a quick, mumbled "hello" before I hurried to find a seat at the back. I needed to be invisible, to avoid any onversation. I didn't want anyone asking questions or trying to welcome me in with their well-meaning niceties. I just wanted to sit quietly, unnoticed, and allow my tears to fall without interruption.

The service began, and though I can't recall the sermon's exact words or the hymns that echoed around me, I do remember the sobbing that overtook me. For the entire hour, silent tears streamed down my face. Every tear was a testament to the overwhelming grief that had built up inside me—for Holly, for my years of suffering, for memories that still haunted me. And the guilt—believing, deep down, that I was the worst mother in the world. Once the service ended, I left without a word—no lingering, no awkward small talk—just out the door, back into the world I had grown so desperate to escape.

But something within me compelled me to return the following week, and the week after that. For six weeks in a row, I would sit at the back, silently weeping through the service, only to vanish into the night as soon as it was over. At first, the words uttered during the sermon felt distant, as if they were meant for someone else, not for a broken soul like mine. Yet, slowly, as each week passed, I began to absorb them. I realised they weren't just old stories or empty rituals; they felt transformative—as though each word were lifting away layers of guilt, shame, and grief that I'd carried for far too long. It was a strange sensation, but a welcome one. I began to feel lighter.

As I continued to attend, I stopped avoiding eye contact with the people around me.

Initially, I had feared judgment, expecting cold stares or whispered criticisms. Instead, I found kindness in their smiles and genuine warmth in their greetings. They welcomed me—not with probing questions or pity, but with quiet understanding and acceptance. Most of them were older, perhaps wise to the ways of the world, and their presence exuded an unwavering faith in something greater than themselves.

There was no judgement here. No one pried into my past or made me feel as though I was beyond saving. Instead, there was a quiet kind of hope—a hope that, gradually, began to seep into my own heart. Slowly, I started to believe that maybe, just maybe, I wasn't irreparably broken.

Yet even as I clung to this fragile hope, another spectre loomed over me—the court case. It hovered like a dark, unyielding cloud, a constant reminder of everything I had endured. The stress was relentless, a crushing weight on my chest that made it nearly impossible to focus on anything else. And then, doubt began to creep back in like a poison. What if I was wrong? What if, by pursuing legal action, I was merely wasting police time? What if Damien had changed?

This thought gnawed at me, twisting itself into my brain like a parasite. I desperately wanted to believe that somewhere, deep down, Damien might be capable of redemption—that all his anger, manipulation, and calculated violence were simply the by-products of stress, poor decisions, and a downward spiral of alcohol-fuelled despair. But could a man like him ever change?

I needed clarity. So, I did something I never imagined I would do—I called his ex. It wasn't for revenge or to swap horror stories; it was for one thing only: closure.

The phone rang, and as soon as she answered, I said, "Look, I just want to say one thing to you, and then we never have to speak again." Her tone was not one of surprise.

Instead, it was calm—almost resigned. "I wondered how long it would take for you to call me," she said softly. "Honestly? I'm surprised you lasted as long as you did with him."

Her words struck me like a blow. I had barely spoken to her before; our only encounters had been carefully orchestrated by Damien himself, a puppet master preventing any genuine connection between us. And she—always concealed behind her sunglasses, even in the dead of winter—had been painted by him as a broken, unreliable addict, someone not to be trusted. And I had believed him. Why wouldn't I?

But now, as I listened to her measured, resilient voice, something shifted inside me.

She didn't sound like the shattered woman he had described. Instead, she was strong—resolute in the aftermath of a lifetime of abuse.

I took a deep, steadying breath, my chest heavy with the burden of unsaid truths. "You probably already know we've split up," I began, my voice shaky with a blend of exhaustion and pain. "But that's not why I'm calling. I just wanted to tell you ...

I won't be driving him around anymore. So, if you see him out and about with your little girl, please be careful." I hesitated, the words tumbling out haltingly. "You probably know, but I'm not sure if you're fully aware—he drinks. A lot."

There was a long, agonising silence on the line. Then, after a breathless pause, she spoke again—a quiet, almost trembling intake of breath that sent a shiver down my spine.

"There's something I need to tell you," she said, and the next words made my stomach churnin horror.

"He hurt me."

My throat constricted as I struggled to find my voice. "I … I didn't know," I whispered. Though I'd been unaware of her allegations against Damien, deep down I had long suspected the truth. I had been blind, either out of denial or sheer exhaustion, choosingnot to see the warning signs.

"I believe you," she continued, her voice barely above a whisper. "He hurt my mumtoo. And my aunt. He pushed my aunt over when he was drunk."

Jesus Christ. I felt bile rising in my throat. I had been with this man—lived with him, slept beside him—and I hadn't truly seen him for who he was. Or had I? Had I simply ignored the signs because the pain was too overwhelming to confront?

But she wasn't finished. "The worst thing he ever did . . ." Her voice broke, and my heart pounded wildly in anticipation of what would come next. I braced myself, dreading the next revelation.

"When I was pregnant," she said, her voice faltering, "he pushed me down the stairs."I gasped, feeling as though the floor had shifted beneath me. In a shaky voice, she continued, "I broke my leg."

My knees buckled, and I had to grasp the edge of the table to steady myself. This wasn't merely a case of a bad temper or a few drunken arguments—it was cold, calculated violence. He could kill, and his actions were deliberate, a terrifying blend of malice and precision.

At that moment, every doubt, and every shred of guilt I had harboured about pressing charges evaporated. I was doing the right thing. There was no redeeming him. I had to ensure that he could hurt no one else. Because if I didn't, he would—without hesitation, without remorse. That was the true nature of Damien: not just dangerous, but evil.

Anger surged through me like a tidal wave—a furious, burning fire ignited by years of suffering, from the early days of school to the torment on that dreadful special bus, from every humiliating moment that chipped away at my self-worth to the relentless abuse inflicted by Damien. How dare he? I was on a mission now and prepared to evoke Clare's Law. I would protect others and perhaps in doing so, I might even change him.

In the UK, there is Clare's Law. I would suggest to any woman dating someone they feel might be a threat: go to the police and ask them about Clare's Law. They can carry out a private check on the person.

It's definitely worth it—you might find out if they're dangerous, and hopefully, it could help protect you or others.

With Damien going to court, I also hoped it might be the wake-up call he needed to change. But deep down, I knew that change was a luxury he would never afford.

I was angry—angry at myself for ever letting him in, for allowing him to manipulate and destroy lives. No more. I vowed then, that with every ounce of strength left in me, I would never stand by and allow his evil to go unchecked.

The phone felt unbearably heavy in my hand, and my pulse thundered in my ears as I whispered, "I'm so sorry." We both knew those words could never undo the damage he had caused. In that charged silence, there was a mutual, unspoken understanding: I wasn't the first to suffer, and if I didn't act, I wouldn't be the last to witness his calculated cruelty.

This wasn't about revenge any longer—it was about stopping him, breaking the cycle of abuse. Damien wasn't just dangerous, he was evil: a cold-hearted force of destruction that needed to be halted. As I listened to her, feeling the weight of every revelation, I knew that I had to do everything in my power to ensure he could never hurt anyone else again.

It was a moment of grim clarity—a realisation that no amount of hope or healing could ever erase the evil that Damien had sown. But it was also a moment that steeled my resolve. I would fight, not just for myself, but for every person whose life he had tainted. Because if I didn't, who would?

CHAPTER TEN:

Starting Over, One Step at a Time

Court. Oh my God—it was terrifying. The mere thought of standing in that dock, knowing I'd have to force my eyes to meet his, sent shivers down my spine. The dread that gripped me was overwhelming; I could barely imagine the moment when I'd be forced to confront the man responsible for so much pain. I had endured countless calls with the court, each one an exercise in preparing myself for what was to come, yet no amount of advice could truly steel me against the reality I was about to face. Every conversation with them brought a fresh wave of anxiety, as the stark reality of the courtroom loomed ever larger in my mind.

They were kind on the phone, patient and understanding, guiding me through every step while explaining the process until I could almost picture it in my head. They even offered me the chance to visit the court in advance—to walk through its halls, to get a feel for the space so that the day itself wouldn't be so daunting. I didn't take them up on that offer, as I'd already done my jury service and knew what to expect. It gave me a strange sort of peace, knowing that both the court and the police were absolutely amazing. They held your hand, so to speak, while being compassionate and caring, walking with you every step of the way. In that support, I found a small measure of strength.

They told me, since I had previously served on a jury, I

should be able to manage—it wouldn't be as terrible as I feared. Still, my heart raced with anxiety, each beat a reminder of the impending confrontation. They even said I could have a screen placed in front of me when giving my evidence, ensuring that I wouldn't have to see him directly. Alternatively, if I had preferred, I could have given my evidence from another room via video link. I wanted to be brave, to face him head-on, to show that I wasn't afraid. But deep down, I knew that my body would betray me—my hands would tremble, my voice would quiver, and my heart would hammer out a rhythm of pure terror.

Then, as if the universe were mocking my inner turmoil, a few days before the scheduled appearance, snow began to fall heavily, blanketing the world in a cold, relentless white. A small, foolish part of me hoped that the snowy chaos might force a postponement—a rescheduling that would allow me more time to prepare, or perhaps a reprieve from the terror altogether. Deep down, I knew that part of that hope was merely a desperate wish to delay the inevitable—the overwhelming fear of facing him in that courtroom.

My mum was terrified too. She didn't want to go, and it broke my heart to see her in such a state, especially as she had already begun showing early signs of dementia—a cruel twist of fate, making her vulnerable. I had hoped it was just stress, but as the days went by, it became painfully clear that her mind was deteriorating. She was already carrying so much of her own burden, and yet, despite everything, she vowed to stand by me. I was grateful beyond words, though her fear only deepened my sorrow.

That snowy morning, we set off on our drive to court. The roads were slick and treacherous, and we left an extra 45 minutes to ensure we wouldn't be late. I couldn't bear the thought of rushing into that courtroom only to face him—my stomach churned at the idea. My mum, her hands shaking uncontrollably and her voice trembling with anxiety, sat beside me in the passenger's seat. I tried to reassure her, but her fear was palpable, an ever-presentshadow that mirrored my own.

As we drew closer—only five minutes away from the imposing building that housed my fate—the weight of the situation pressed down on me like a mighty force. I struggled to stay calm for my mum's sake, but inside, I was a wreck of nerves and dread. I phoned the court to confirm our arrival, to ensure that everything was on track, but a voice on the otherend of the line had frozen me in place.

"We'll check your details," the voice said, its tone measured. After what felt like an eternity, the reply came: "The case is cancelled today. We're not sure why, but it's related toDamien."

At that moment, my heart dropped: relief and confusion collided in a maelstrom of emotion. Relief because I wouldn't have to come face-to-face with him that day—the thoughtof his calculated, cold-blooded cruelty was almost too much to bear. And confusion, with everything having built up to this moment, only to fizzle out with a single phone call. I had no idea what Damien had done to prompt the cancellation, only that the case was far from over.

"They'll be in touch," the man on the phone added, his voice trailing off into silence. I ended the call, my mind still reeling from the unexpected news. I turned to my mum, who sat silently by the window, her face pale and her hands clasped tightly in her lap. The tension in the car was overwhelming.

For now, the battle had been postponed. But as I stared out at the falling snow, a heavy realisation settled in—this was not the end of the war. The postponement was merely a delay, a brief interlude before the inevitable confrontation. As we drove away from the court that snowy morning, my mind was awash with a tumult of emotions—relief, anger, confusion, and an unyielding determination that the war against him was far from over.

I knew I had to rebuild my life. Again.

It was a feeling I knew all too well—starting over from nothing, clawing my way back when every ounce of energy had been spent on surviving the previous nightmare. The exhaustion wasn't just physical; it seeped deep into my bones, into my very soul. But what choice did I have? I had to put my head down and start again, no matter how broken I felt.

Someone once suggested I see a doctor, but I laughed bitterly. How was a doctor supposed to mend a shattered heart? Could they prescribe a remedy for exhaustion? For the crushing weight of having to begin again when I could barely force myself out of bed. No. Deep down, I knew the only way forward was through the storm. I had to get up, show up, and rebuild—not just for me, but for my son and everyone placed in harm's way of Damien.

Then, out of the blue, my parents dropped a bombshell. They told me they had decided to sell up and move away—not just down the road, but nearly 200 miles away. I was in shock. It felt as if the support blanket I'd come to rely on had been ripped away in an instant. I was hurt and upset, and a part of me just screamed, "WTF?" All at once, I realised I had to get my life sorted—and fast.

Living with my parents was only ever meant to be temporary, and time was slipping away like sand through my fingers.

It was absolute madness. I began searching for jobs, but the irony was cruel enough to be a sick joke—a twisted version of Groundhog Day. The application forms were torture: page after page of repetitive, mind-numbing questions. Being dyslexic, half of the multiple-choice options seemed equally plausible, yet that wasn't even the worst part. The real problem was that my brain was utterly fried. I couldn't think. I didn't want to think. My mind was too exhausted to process anything beyond the sheer act of survival.

So, I applied for anything—any job that would take me in, anything that would pay the bills and offer even a glimmer of security. Within weeks, I found myself doing cleaning jobs. The hours were brutal—starting at 5 a.m., working six days a week—but I had no choice. I had to take whatever was offered. It was degrading, scrubbing floors on my hands and knees for seven endless hours, sweat trickling down my back, my body aching with every movement. But it didn't matter; I had to keep going.

One job wasn't enough, so I took another. Then another. My days blurred into an endless cycle of work, exhaustion, and barely a moment to breathe. I'd finish one shift and drive straight to the next, my limbs heavy and my eyes stinging from a lack of sleep. If I was lucky, I'd steal two hours to myself in the middle of the day—just enough time to devour a sandwich and close my eyes for a few precious minutes before dragging myself back into the grind.

I looked like a mess, I felt like a mess, but I didn't care. I had a goal: to save enough money for a deposit, to secure a home, to give my son the stability he deserved. But the money was pitiful—barely enough to scrape by—and the debts . . . they were suffocating. The relentless calls from creditors never ceased. Some were aggressive and harsh, their voices slicing through the phone with demands for payment. Others were softer, inquiring about my mental health while trying to work out a payment plan. Yet, no matter what, the numbers never balanced—more money was going out than coming in. It became a constant, desperate balancing act, a relentless game of survival. Meanwhile, my parents were in the process of selling their house—a stark reminder that time was running out. The pressure wasunbearable.

And then, just when I thought I could push it all to the back of my mind, the newcourt date arrived.

The moment I saw the letter, my stomach twisted into knots. I had managed to ignore it for a while—distracting myself with work, with the relentless act of survival—but now it was all too real. I would have to face him.

I had proof. I had done nothing wrong, I kept telling myself that. Yet, the fear remained—the dread of the unknown, of what he might be like in court. Would he try to intimidate me? Would he smirk, that cold, calculated smirk he always wore when he thoughthe had the upper hand? And then I wondered—why was I so scared? All I had ever done was try to help him. I had given him everything, and yet here I was, picking up the shattered pieces of my life while he carried on, untouched and unrepentant. No one could help him—not the police, not his family. Only Damien could help himself.

And then, amid the chaos, I came across a poem. It hit me like a physical blow, rightbetween the heart. It was raw, brutal, and unflinching in its truth. It wasn't my own writing, yet it resonated with me on a profound level. Its title screamed at me:

I NEED To Get Drunk (warning—brutal honesty)

I am not your child, spouse, or friend. I've changed. I don't belong to you anymore. I don't care about you—not in the way you want me to. I care about getting drunk. I WANT to get drunk. I will do ANYTHING to get drunk. I LOVE getting drunk. I NEED to get drunk . . .and I will step over you to do it.

When I look at you, I don't see YOU. I see a means to an end. You have money. I want it. End of story. I don't care if you can't pay the rent. I don't care if you need groceries. I don't care if you promised you wouldn't give me money again. I don't care if you lie to Dad. I don't care if you're broke. Sell your rings, take a loan, sell your electronics, max out your credit cards, borrow the money from someone else—because if you don't, I will STEAL it. I WILL find a way to get DRUNK.

If you think you can CHANGE me or SAVE me. You are WRONG! Something cold and dead slithers within me now. I no longer respond to love or truth. You can CRY all you want—I don't care. I have no integrity or values; my morals are relics of a bygone era. I will say anything, do anything, and hurt anyone to get my next DRINK.

Although I may play the game with you, make no mistake—I don't play it because I LOVE you. I play it because I want my BOOZE. I will say whatever you want to hear, promise you the world, look you in the eyes, and then shatter your heart. Over and over again. I no longer possess a heart—I have a HUNGER. It's calculating, and manipulative, and it OWNS me.

Strangely, you're thankful for this hunger. For when I feel it rising, I find you—quickly. Then, after I've extracted everything, I want, I leave you bereft. You're left anxious and desperate, offering to buy my food or pay my rent. You always GIVE me something.

By now, your NEED is almost as great as mine. I can't

remain SICK without you, and you can't breathe without ME.

You think you're helping me. You believe you're making a difference, but deep down, you know what you're really doing... you're enabling my ALCOHOLISM.

I won't say it outright, but you know it, deep down. If we continue like this, one or both of us will die—me from a broken body, a car crash, or a suicide you paid for, and you from a heart attack or stroke.

You'll wait YEARS for me to change or see the light, and I will take full advantage of that. You keep my secrets and protect my lies. You clean up my messes and bail me out. You love me to the exclusion of EVERYONE else. You harbour bitterness and resentment. You hide from your friends and isolate yourself. You HATE. Your world revolves around one thing only

ME.

But will your LOVE ever become greater than your FEAR? Would you be strong enough to reach out for help? Will you learn to say NO? Will you allow me to face the consequences of my actions? Will you LOVE me enough to endure your own discomfort and finally stop enabling my addiction?

I lay trapped within the coils of this cold, dark serpent called alcoholism—and I am . ... dying.

This brutal honesty, this truth of his addiction, was the moment I truly began my healing journey. It was when I decided to go within, to do the inner work. I had spent so long merely surviving, relentlessly pushing forward, that I'd never stopped to acknowledge the depth of my wounds. I realised I couldn't keep carrying all this pain; it was weighing me down, poisoning me from the inside out.

I didn't have much money, but I was resourceful. I reached out to a therapist and offered a trade—I would help her with my skills for free if she would help me heal. To myrelief, she agreed. And so, I began peeling back the layers, one by one.

At first, it was terrifying. Opening that box—the one I had kept sealed for so long—felt akin to ripping open an old wound, letting every painful memory surge to the surface. I had to piece it together, bit by bit—how had I come to this? The sadness, the grief,the humiliation, the loss—it was overwhelming. Yet for the first time, I was in a safe space, and I allowed myself to feel it all.

Then, something incredible happened. Healing became . . . addictive. The more I worked through the pain, the more I wanted to heal. Every breakthrough brought a sense offreedom, a lightness I hadn't known in years. It was as though I was reclaiming the parts ofmyself, I had lost. I became obsessed with learning more, with understanding more, with going ever deeper. I even trained in Reiki, feeling a strange sense of familiarity—as if I had done this before in another lifetime. Then I moved on to exploring the Akashic Records,eager to uncover yet more layers of healing.

Healing was like peeling an onion—layer after layer, each one revealing somethingnew. And with every wound I healed, I felt stronger, lighter, more whole.

But healing didn't erase the daily struggles. I was still exhausted—still waking at 5 a.m., still working endless hours just to keep afloat. I had to push past my own embarrassment. One day, I looked down at my trainers—my only pair. The hole in them had grown so big that my toes poked through. They weren't even trainers anymore; they resembled flimsy flip-flops barely holding together. Once, I would have been mortified, headbowed, hoping no one would notice. But something had changed. Now, when people stared, Iheld my head high.

Because I was proud. Proud of the person I was becoming. Proud that I was still standing, still fighting, still rebuilding from nothing. And for the first time in a long time, I started to feel something I never thought I would again—I began to love myself. Even if itwas just a little.

The court date was inching ever closer. I had only a few weeks left, and strangely, amidst the chaos, I began to feel a sliver of calm. I reminded myself that I had people in mycorner—people who supported me and believed in my truth. Why should I be afraid? I had done nothing wrong. And yet, a small, persistent tremor of fear remained at the thought of standing in that courtroom, facing him with all its attendant terror.

But I wasn't doing this solely for myself. I was doing it for every soul he had hurt, foranyone who might cross his path in the future. Maybe—just maybe—this would be the wake-up call he needed. Perhaps it would force him to change his ways, even if only a little. Who was I kidding? Would he ever change? Probably not. Yet, I clung to the hope that he might, if not for himself, then for his family, for all the people who had suffered in his wake.

Two days before the court date, anxiety began to creep in again. My stomach churned; my hands trembled with a nervous energy that I couldn't quite shake off. And then, out of theblue, I got the call.

"It's been cancelled."I felt my breath hitch.

"Cancelled?" I managed to croak out, disbelief colouring my voice.

"Yes. Due to personal circumstances—Damien can't attend,"

the voice replied flatly.

Personal circumstances? What could that possibly mean? They offered no further explanation, only that the case would be rescheduled.

I hung up the phone, feeling the familiar mixture of relief and frustration wash over me. Relief because, at least for today, I wouldn't have to face him in that stifling courtroom; frustration because it felt like all my efforts had been building up to this moment, only for it to fizzle out into more waiting and uncertainty. The endless delays, the constant cloud of anticipation and dread—it was all utterly exhausting, draining every bit of hope I had managed to cling to.

But I couldn't let this setback put my life on hold indefinitely. I had to keep going. And so, I did.

***

For months after, I found myself lost in thought, questioning what I truly wanted to do with my life. I knew I wanted to help people, to make a genuine difference in the world, but the pressing question was—how? It felt almost surreal to even ask myself that, considering where I had come from. I remembered the kid on the special bus, the one who struggled to read or write, constantly battling a system that never seemed to understand. And yet, here I was, realising that the very weaknesses that once defined me were slowly transforming into my greatest strengths.

I had fallen in love with writing.

The idea of writing a book was both daunting and exhilarating. If my story could resonate with even one person—if it could offer a sliver of hope to someone drowning in their own despair—then every ounce of pain would have been worth it. But

146

as I let my mind wander further, a bigger picture emerged—one that extended far beyond my own words.

Everywhere I turned, it was saturated with negativity—fear-driven headlines and stories designed to keep people trapped in a cycle of worry and doubt. But what if I could change that narrative? What if, instead of feeding people fear, I could offer them hope?

That's when the idea hit me.

Why couldn't there be a magazine dedicated to uplifting, empowering, and inspiring people? A place where readers could find not just expert advice, tips, and insights, but also authentic stories of resilience, courage, and transformation. Stories like mine. Stories that serve as a reminder that no matter how engulfing the darkness, there is always a glimmer of light waiting to break through.

Of course, people laughed at the idea. "You're mad," they said. Perhaps I was. But I had never been one to choose the easy path, and if I was going to do something, it had to be something profound.

So, I threw myself into months of research. I spoke to store owners, supermarket managers, and everyday people—asking them what kind of magazines they actually read. Some yearned for a glossy escape into the worlds of fashion and beauty, while others sought business insights, financial tips, and educational content to improve their lives. And then there were those who longed for something deeper—real stories of hope and perseverance that could inspire them to step beyond their fears and take action in their own lives.

That's when Mind Jump Magazine was born.

People often asked me what the name meant. I'd smile softly and reply, "It's exactly what it says. So many of us, including myself, have been stuck in fear—trapped by our own doubts and limitations. This magazine is about taking that leap, about jumping out of fear andinto something greater." In those words, I hoped to capture the essence of what I wanted to create: a platform where we could all share our struggles, our breakthroughs, and our dreams,unashamed and unfiltered.

At that moment, with the court date postponed and my life caught in a state of perpetual uncertainty, I found solace in the idea of building a space for change—a sanctuary where hope could triumph over fear. Every page, every article, every story would be an invitation to rebuild, to transform, and to leap into a brighter future. I knew in my gut that this wasn't just a passion project—it was my destiny. I had to create something beautiful, something that could serve as a vessel for the stories that needed to be told. Stories like JC's:

John's Socks—A Heart-Melting Story

It was the crisp autumn of 2016 when John's journey truly began. John, who had Down syndrome, never allowed his condition to define him or hold him back. In his final year of school at Huntington High and Wilson Tech—where he diligently studied retailing and customer service—he faced the looming question of what would come next. At the same time, his father, Mark, was busy exploring online business ventures, always on the lookout for new opportunities. As school came to an end, John was confronted with a daunting decision: What kind of future did he want to create for himself?

The options before him felt uninspiring and lacked the spark that he craved. They didn't excite him; they didn't speak to his creative soul. One day, with a spark in his eye that hinted at a bold idea, he turned to his father and said something that would changeeverything: "I want to go into business with you."

John had already experienced working alongside Mark, and he knew deep down thatthe best way to find a job he would truly love was to create one himself. Mark, recognising the fire in his son, agreed without hesitation. But there was one glaring problem—they needed an idea that resonated with both of them.

John's first suggestion was a fun store. "I wanted something fun and creative," he explained with a hopeful grin. Yet, try as they might, neither of them could quite pin down what a "fun store" would actually sell. The idea felt too vague, too intangible to take root.

Next, John suggested a food truck, inspired by the film *Chef*, which told the heartwarming tale of a father and son duo running a food truck together. It seemed like the perfect blend of passion and practicality—until they confronted a simple, unassailable truth."We can't cook," John admitted with a sheepish laugh, and the idea dissolved before their eyes.

Then, in a moment of sudden clarity—a true eureka moment—John's eyes lit up.

"Let's sell socks," he declared. "Crazy socks." It was as if the answer had been waiting forhim all along. He already had a name in mind and had even sketched out ideas for the website. When pressed on why socks, John's answer was simple and pure: "I've worn crazysocks my entire life. They're fun, colourful, and creative. They let me be me."

Mark couldn't help but smile. At that moment, he realised that John's idea wasn't just a random spark—it was deeply personal. "John has always loved fun socks," Mark recalled warmly. "We'd drive around together searching for the most outrageous, whimsical designs. It made me think that if he loved them this much, surely others would too."

And so, they set to work. They built a website using Shopify, painstakingly convinced suppliers to trust them with their inventory and navigated the maze of filing the necessary paperwork. Their marketing plan was refreshingly simple—a Facebook page coupled with a few low-quality yet earnest videos featuring John animatedly talking about his love for socks. It was during one of these videos that John coined his now-famous catchphrase: "Socks, socks, and more socks!"

The launch day was set for 10 a.m., but as fate would have it, the website crashed. They waited, anxious and hopeful, until finally, at 3 p.m., the site went live. And then, they waited. It wasn't long before orders began rolling in. At first, the support came from their local community—friends, neighbours, and others who had seen John's infectious enthusiasm on social media.

John wanted every delivery to be special. Instead of merely shipping the socks in standard packaging, he placed them in bright red boxes, added a few pieces of candy, and included a handwritten thank-you note. Then, with a sincerity that only he could muster, he would personally deliver these parcels to customers' doors. People loved it. They took photos with John and flaunted their new socks on social media. Word of John's Crazy Socks spread like wildfire.

By the end of that first month, John's Crazy Socks had shipped 452 orders and generated over $13,000 in revenue. What started as a small, hopeful idea—a way for John to carve out a future that was entirely his own—quickly blossomed into something extraordinary. Today, John's Crazy Socks stands as the largest sock distributor in the world. And to think, it all began with a simple idea, a dash of courage, and a father who believed inhis son's vision.

Why This Story Matters:

John's story is not just about socks—it's about defying limitations. Despite having Down syndrome, John never allowed himself to be defined by his condition. Instead of waiting for an opportunity to knock, he created his own door. He transformed his love for crazy socks into a thriving business that not only changed his own life but also brought joy and inspiration to countless others. When I first heard John's story, it melted my heart. It wasexactly the kind of story I yearned to share—a story of hope, determination, and undeniable proof that dreams can blossom, no matter where you start.

That's when I knew Mind Jump Magazine had to exist. Not just to share stories like John's, but to remind people of what is possible when we dare to leap out of fear and into something greater. This wasn't merely about publishing a magazine—it was about changing lives, about sparking a movement of hope and transformation. It was then I realised my journey had truly begun.

CHAPTER ELEVEN:

The Journey from Hell

As you grow up, you come to realise that love isn't always spoken—it's often shown in subtle, sometimes unrecognisable ways that only reveal their true depth in hindsight. For me, love was everything. It was the essence I craved, the elusive treasure I chased, the energy I longed to pour into others, especially after so many moments in life when I felt utterly alone.

My dad, in his own pragmatic way, demonstrated love through action—by ensuring we had a roof over our heads, by working tirelessly, and by providing for us. But words?

Conversations? Genuine emotion? Those were foreign concepts to him. I had spent my whole life trying to reach out to him, trying to break through his stoic façade, but he would merely grunt, as though each word had a price. So, when I heard about my dad's mum, my paternal nan and her imminent passing, I knew the news would hit him harder than it did anyone else.

I went to see him, expecting the usual: his silent, withdrawn manner, his stoic dedication to work as a shield against pain. At the time, he was in his seventies and still grafting away, clinging to what he knew best as his way of coping. Perhaps I had inherited that same relentless drive—throwing myself into work when life became unbearable. But this time, I couldn't let him bury his grief beneath his endless labour.

"We're going to see Nan," I told him, my voice steady and resolute.

At first, he didn't even look up—just shook his head and clenched his jaw, as if themere thought of facing this loss was too overwhelming. "I can't. I just can't do it," he muttered, the words heavy with resignation.

Then, at that very moment, something happened that I had never witnessed in my entire life. His body began to tremble; his strong, burdened shoulders slumped, and for the first time, he broke down completely. Tears, long held at bay behind a mask of iron resolve, streamed down his face. I was stunned—this was the man who had drilled into me that one must never show weakness, who always recited the Queen's mantra: "Never explain, never complain." Yet here he was, overwhelmed by more than sixty years of accumulated pain and emotion, finally giving way to grief.

I sat with him in silence, offering no words, no empty platitudes—just a presence, allowing him this raw, unfiltered moment of vulnerability. Time seemed to stretch, each second laden with unspoken sorrow, until finally, he sniffled, wiped his face with his sleeve, and, with a quiet determination that belied his earlier collapse, said, "We'll go in the morning."

That was it. No grand speeches, no profound revelations—just a simple, heartfelt statement. And yet, that was enough. In that fragile moment, I understood that love was not measured by eloquent words or dramatic gestures, but by the quiet bravery of showing up, ofbeing there when it mattered most.

***

The next morning, I braced myself for what would be a long, awkward, silent car ride—sevenor eight hours trapped with a man

I had probably, in my entire life, exchanged barely two hours of words with. My dad and I had never been close. I'd been living under his roof—an arrangement I was utterly grateful for, given he didn't have to take me in—but we hardly spoke a word. I kept to myself most of the time, retreating into my bedroom to work on the business, only emerging to grab food or work. Night after night, I'd lock myself away to labour over the magazine, so as you can imagine, I was absolutely dreading this ride.

As soon as I climbed into the car, I turned to him and said, "I need to speak to you." He merely nodded, and before I could utter another word, he cut in with his familiar, dismissive tone and asked, "When are you going to get a proper job?"

Those were his only words—a refrain he'd repeated so often that I knew his idea of a "proper job" was something old-fashioned, like being a nurse or a secretary. Neither of which were ever meant for me.

I inhaled sharply. Here we go, I thought.

"Stop right there," I shot back. "You're going to listen. We have a long drive ahead, and you need to know everything—why I left my ex-husband, why I left Damien, everything I've been through."

And so, for nearly three hours straight, I talked. I unloaded years of pent-up pain, frustration, and experiences he had no inkling about. I told him about the hardships I had endured, the mistakes I'd made, and the lessons I had painfully learned along the way. I needed him to understand, to see the scars beneath my silence.

By the time I was done, I felt lighter—as if I'd exhaled a lifetime of grief and regret. And for the first time in my life, my dad didn't dismiss me. He didn't shut me out. He just listened—truly listened.

Something shifted in that car that day. The person I once was—the girl who had allowed people to walk all over her, who stayed silent just to keep the peace—was gone. Lifehad tempered me and hardened me in the best possible way. I was no longer afraid to stand up for myself. I had built something magnificent from the ashes of my past, and for the first time, I sensed that perhaps, deep down, my dad was too.

Once we'd reached our destination, it was as if decades of silence had been rewritten with understanding. It wasn't perfect, but it was a start. And at that moment, I realized something profound—I wasn't angry at him anymore. For so long, I had resented the fact thathe never stepped in, never offered a lifeline when I was drowning. But as I sat there, a new perspective dawned on me.

Had he helped me and made my life easier, would I have ever found the strength to stand on my own? Or would I have ended up dependent on him, falling into another suffocating, controlling relationship? I think, deep down, he knew that I needed to find my own path. And maybe, in his own unspoken way, he had been proud of me all along, but Iwould never know.

I had spent years feeling that the world wouldn't give me a chance, and that life wasinherently unfair. But sitting there in that car, amidst shared silence and raw revelations, I understood the truth: no one owed me a damn thing. I had my health, my two feet, and the burning determination to build a life I was proud of. If I hadn't walked the path I did, my magazine wouldn't exist. My purpose wouldn't exist. I wouldn't be here. And this was exactly where I was meant to be.

When we finally arrived at the hospice, it felt surreal—like stepping into a place both frozen in time and hurtling forward all at once. It was miles away from anything familiar, and I hadn't seen Nan in years. The woman lying in that bed was not the vibrant figure of my memories. She had changed.

She wasn't the strong, sharp, distant matriarch I recalled. Instead, she was frail, almost weightless against the stark white hospital sheets. Her once steady, capable hands now trembled as I reached out to hold them. In that fragile moment, something unexpected occurred. It was . . . peaceful.

I had never really had a close relationship with my paternal nan. And my dad? His connection with her was even more distant—a man haunted by his own past wounds, too detached to allow any warmth to seep through. That was why we rarely saw her; he carried his own pain, and perhaps he never wanted to. There was no tenderness in his voice when he mentioned her, no longing to reconnect. Just cold, clinical detachment.

But as I sat beside her, something shifted. In that quiet, vulnerable moment, she was not the woman of my childhood or his memories. She was simply a human being—fragile and exposed—reaching out, silently asking for comfort, for a moment of shared solace.

I stayed with her for about 20 minutes, fully aware that this was not my moment to grieve alone. This was my dad's moment—a time for him to confront his buried emotions and regrets. And as I sat there, holding her trembling hand, I realised that sometimes, love is shown in the breaking of silence, in the shared tears of a long-hidden sorrow.

It was hard—gut-wrenchingly hard—to watch the past unravel in real-time, to witness the breaking of a man who had always preached stoicism and strength. But it was real. And for that moment, as the weight of years seemed to lift just a little, I understood that even the toughest souls can be softened by loss.

I knew then that the journey from hell was far from over, but it was one I no longer had to walk alone. And even in that painful, fragile space between grief and hope, there was the promise of a new beginning.

I could see my dad's relief before we'd even walked into the hospice—his hesitation, the silent battle raging within. He didn't want to be there; he was terrified of facing her, of confronting all the unsaid words and buried memories between them. And yet, he did.

When he finally stepped out of that room, something in him had shifted. There was a quiet relief in his eyes—a subtle light that hinted he had found a measure of peace, even if just for a moment. I searched his face for any sign of what he was feeling. "Are you okay?" I asked softly, my voice trembling with concern.

"Yep," he replied, short and to the point—just a single word that carried a world of meaning. It was all I was going to get from him. And honestly, I didn't need more.

Deep down, I knew. I knew in that fragile moment, something had been healed inside him—something he would never admit, something he would never fully put into words. I was just grateful he had found the courage to go in. If he hadn't, I was certain he would have carried that regret for the rest of his life.

Strangely, my nan didn't pass away right then. The doctors had said she had days to live, yet she clung on for months—perhaps because she, too, had unfinished business, unresolved emotions that kept her tethered to this world. But that moment in the room between my dad and his mother had already served its purpose. It had mended something deep within them, a healing that no number of words could ever replicate.

What I hadn't expected was how profoundly it healed me, too. That journey wasn't solely about me. It was about my dad and my nan finding a semblance of peace before it was too late. But in the process, something shifted between my ad and me. We were never the kind of father and daughter who called each other every day or exchanged tight embraces.

That wasn't who we were—and perhaps, we never would be.

Yet now, we understand each other more. We would never be inseparable or overly sentimental, but I sensed a softening of the barriers that had long separated us. Deep down, I think he might regret some of the years we lost, the missed opportunities for warmth and connection. Still, I wouldn't change a thing. Before we come into this world, I believe we choose our parents—and if I had the choice, I would still have chosen him. The lessons he taught me, though harsh and often delivered in a cold manner, weren't born out of cruelty. They were the hard truths of survival.

Were they harsh? Yes.

Were they painful? Absolutely.

But did they shape me? More than anything else.

As I sit here now, tears quietly falling while writing these words, I feel an overwhelming gratitude. Grateful for every lesson, each challenge, and every moment of struggle that shaped my inner strength. And in that gratitude, my purpose revealed itself.

But life doesn't often pause for reflection. The world keeps moving, and so do I. That journey with my dad and my nan changed something deep inside me—a raw, profound shift.

Seeing my dad finally break down, confronting decades of pent-up emotion, was like witnessing a secret being released. Those tears weren't just for my nan; they were for all the hurt he had carried, for every moment of pain that had been locked away inside him for as long as I could remember.

That day, while sitting in the silence of the room, I spoke to my dad about how I had felt as a child—the little kid who yearned for love, even if it was delivered in his own unconventional way. At that moment, the walls of pain and misunderstanding crumbled, releasing years of sorrow in a single, cathartic instant as if by finally giving voice to all the emotions that had been building up inside me, I uncovered an unexpected sense of peace.

That raw, honest conversation, that shared moment of vulnerability, brought us closer in a way that transcended words. It wasn't about changing the past—it was about healing from it, accepting the scars as part of our journey. And as I reflect on that day now, I understand that sometimes the most profound healing comes not from grand gestures or elaborate apologies, but from the simple act of being present, of listening, and of finally allowing ourselves to feel.

But just like that, the healing hit pause and the crushing reality of life pressed in once again, relentless and unyielding. I was back to scrubbing floors until my hands felt raw, back to stacking shelves with a weariness that seeped into my bones. It wasn't glamorous, and it certainly wasn't the life I had once envisioned in my wildest dreams. Yet, the bills still had to be paid, and the world, indifferent to my inner turmoil, kept spinning on.

The days dragged on slowly, each one a reminder of the endless routine of my existence. Weeks passed in a blur of monotonous work and fleeting moments of solitude. I wasn't sure where to turn anymore, but I forced myself to keep moving—one agonising, uncertain step after the other—clinging to the desperate hope that someday I would find a way forward.

Then, one evening, my phone rang unexpectedly. The shrill ring cut through the silence of my small flat, and I answered to hear the trembling voice of my friend. She was tearing herself apart over a situation spiralling completely out of control. I could hear the panic and desperation in her voice—the raw emotion of someone who felt utterly abandoned by the world. She had no money to feed her children; the payments from her work were late, and she felt trapped with nowhere else to turn.

I knew all too well what it felt like to be stuck on the edge, with nothing but a few scraps of hope to cling to. In that instant, without hesitation, I did what little I could. I sent her the last of the money in my account—the scant few pounds I had left. It wasn't much, but it was something. It was a lifeline thrown into a stormy sea, and I hoped it might help her, even if only just a little.

After I hung up, I sat there for a long moment, staring at the empty cup of tea in front of me. Its warmth had long since faded, yet I clutched it as if its residual heat could somehow offer comfort or solace. But the truth was, I wasn't sure I was helping anyone—perhaps not even myself. I had just given away my last bit of money, and deep down, I knew I was barely scraping by. There was a gnawing fear inside me, an ever-present unease that whispered I might not be as strong as I liked to believe.

But then, as I sat there in the quiet, I thought of my friend— of the hope that my small act might enable her to buy food for her children, to experience a moment of relief in the midst of her struggle. I remembered what it felt like to have nothing—to be invisible, to feel utterly uncared for. In that reflection, a fragile certainty blossomed within me: this was why Ikept going.

I wasn't just here to survive; I was here to make a difference. I was determined to help others survive too, even when I was barely holding on myself. Because, in the end, it isn't about what you have. It's about what you give, however little it may be.

Taking a deep, steadying breath, I finished my now-cold tea and forced myself back to work. I wiped away the doubts, pushed aside the lingering despair, and set about my tasks with renewed determination. I wasn't merely here to exist—I was here to leave my mark, to be a beacon of hope amid the shadows.

That night, as I lay in bed beneath a threadbare duvet, I found myself staring at the vision board I had made months ago. Back when hope still fluttered in my heart, I had filled that board with dreams, plans, and stories I longed to share. In the centre, the words "Mind Jump" and "Dating App Goddess" were scrawled in bold letters, surrounded by a jumble of ideas and aspirations. Over time, the board had collected dust, buried beneath piles of unpaid bills and unopened letters, nearly forgotten in the relentless march of everyday struggles.

Yet now, something within me reignited. I realised that I had spent so long waiting for the perfect time—the right opportunity, the perfect break—to move forward. But what if there was no perfect time at all? What if the only way to break free from this cycle was to simply start—right here, right now, with whatever little I had left?

I reached for my battered notebook and began to write again. I poured out my thoughts, my pain, and my dreams onto the pages. I wrote about struggle and resilience, about finding hope in the darkest moments, and about the beauty of real life—raw, unfiltered, and sometimes painfully honest. I wrote because people needed to hear it. They needed to know that they weren't alone in their battles, that even in the depths of despair, there was a spark waiting to be fanned into a flame.

As I sat there, pen in hand and heart pounding with a newfound purpose, I knew this was only the beginning. Each word I wrote was a step forward—a defiant leap out of fear and into a future where I could truly make a difference. I wrote not just to survive, but to transform pain into purpose, to turn every hardship into a story of hope and resilience.

At that moment, as I filled page after page with my truth, I realised my journey, with all its setbacks and small victories, was exactly where I was meant to be. The healing might pause sometimes, and the weight of reality might press in relentlessly, but I kept moving. I would keep giving, keep creating, and keep fighting—not just for myself, but for everyone who needed a reminder that even in the darkest times, there is a way forward.

And so, with every written word, I took another step out of the shadows, determined to light the way for others and for myself. This was just the beginning—a promise to rise again, to leap into the unknown, and to create a life of meaning, no matter how hard the journey might be.

CHAPTER TWELVE:

Could This Be My Lucky Break?

The journey with the magazine had begun. But it wasn't glamorous—it was gruelling, relentless, and downright soul-crushing at times. For six long months, I reached out to every connection I had, begging and pleading just to get some big names to grace the covers. Every day was like I was standing on the edge of something great, yet I could never quite grab hold of it. I hustled constantly, chasing down opportunities, and arranging meetings in London, all while scrubbing floors until my hands were raw and stacking shelves in a never-ending cycle of labour. No matter how hard I worked, it felt as if I was drowning in the grind.

I'd wake up at 5 a.m. and wouldn't get home until late at night—sometimes not until 11 or midnight—and by then, I was still burning the midnight oil on the magazine. There was simply no time for rest, no space to breathe or to dream. The fantasy of lying on a warm beach, letting the sun caress my weary body and mind, seemed impossibly far away. Every minute was a battle against exhaustion as I built this company brick by painstaking brick, article by article.

In the gaps between scrubbing floors and dusting off shelves, I would call in experts to help me write content, reaching out to anyone who might be willing to contribute to this fledgling project. Even as I immersed myself in the minutiae of cleaning, my mind raced with ideas for the magazine—ways to make it known, to get it out there, to make it something real and tangible. Yet, I had nothing—no money, no security, just the hope that somehow it would all fall into place. And, as if that wasn't enough, there was the constant pressure gnawing at me in the back of my mind: Mum and Dad were moving, not up the road, but 200 miles away and I still needed to raise enough money for a deposit and rent. Every day, the weight of responsibility pressed down harder.

Then reality set in. My life had become entirely consumed by work—work and more work. I was so tired, so utterly drained, yet amidst all the struggle, the magazine was finally starting to take shape. People were beginning to recognise it, even without enough money to back it up. I couldn't even cover the most basic of needs. The roof I've been trying to keep over my son's and my head was literally being sold, and I found myself constantly searching for a way to change our circumstances.

One of the girls I worked with mentioned that the government might be able to help but asking for help was something I loathed. I wasn't one to swallow my pride easily, but I had no choice. I didn't have a deposit to rent a house, and no other option was in sight. So, with a mixture of trepidation and desperation, I contacted them.

I'll never forget walking into that government office—humiliated, embarrassed, and feeling like a complete failure. The security guards eyed me with suspicion, as though I didn't belong there, and honestly, I couldn't blame them. I asked the two guards why they were stationed there, and they explained it was because of the abuse they sometimes endured from people in similar desperate situations. Their words shocked me; it was a harsh reminderof how rough life could get.

I then went upstairs for my meeting, unable to hold back the tears any longer.

Whether it was embarrassment at how my life had crumbled or the crushing weight of everything coming together, I couldn't stop the flood of emotions. My life resembled a tragic movie—a bad soap opera unfolding before my eyes. But then, the man in the office greeted me with kindness. He handed me tissues, told me how refreshing it was to see someone so sincere, and reassured me that they could indeed help. I left that office with a glimmer of hope, though a deep sense of shame still gnawed at me.

After weeks of identification checks and waiting, they finally confirmed that they could help me—provided I secured some form of accommodation, even if it was only temporary. I started looking, but it seemed no one wanted to take on someone like me.

Despite working honest days with two jobs, the money I brought in was never enough. It was maddening—no matter how hard I worked, I couldn't pay the bills, buy food, or simply live. I often wondered, with bitter frustration, what the world had come to. People worked tirelessly,paying taxes and national insurance, yet so many, including my colleagues, struggled to afford even a modest Christmas present or manage the unexpected expense of a broken car. It was a heartbreaking cycle; a constant reminder of how unfair life could be.

I knew I had to change my situation. So, I decided not to tell the letting agent I was on some form of support, and I found a place where I didn't need to pay a deposit. I could hardly believe it—God was looking after me in some inexplicable way. I went to view the place, andit was as if the universe had performed a small miracle. It wasn't mine yet, but it was something. It meant I would have a roof over my son's head—a symbol of hope and survival. That alone was worth everything. I was proud of that moment. I'd gone from having nothing to having something, and it wasn't just a house—it was a fresh start.

For the first time in so long, I felt a sense of security. I had real floors beneath my feet, and soft carpets in rooms that had once been barren, and for my son, that was everything. It was a new beginning—a tangible sign that I could, indeed, rebuild my life.

Over the ensuing months, I continued to work relentlessly on the magazine. I juggled cleaning and stacking shelves, grinding away from 5:30 a.m. until late at night. It was soul-sapping work, but I had a goal now. I had my son to care for, and I had the magazine—a project that represented my passion and my resilience. Every morning, as I woke up in a place with soft carpet underfoot—a luxury I'd never known before—I felt a renewed sense of purpose.

But as the months wore on, I realised I couldn't keep doing it all by myself. I needed help to grow, to expand my vision, and to take the next step. Between shifts, while I was bone-tired and barely holding on, I worked on a pitch deck for the dating app and the magazine. Every spare moment was dedicated to refining my ideas and reaching out for support. For three long months, I sent that pitch deck to over 3,300 investors, hoping that one of them would see the spark in my project and help turn my relentless hustle into something sustainable.

It was a journey of endless struggle, of battling exhaustion and despair every single day. Yet, with every pitch sent, with every rejection and every small victory, I felt that spark of possibility growing inside me. The magazine, once just a glimmer in the darkness, was slowly becoming a beacon of hope—a testament to the power of resilience and the unyielding drive to create something beautiful out of chaos.

I knew then that my journey was far from over. Every moment of hardship, every sleepless night, every tear shed in quiet desperation had led me to this point. And though the road ahead was still uncertain and filled with obstacles, I had already begun to build something remarkable. I wasn't just surviving; I was fighting for a better future—one article, one connection, one small breakthrough at a time.

Do you know how many responses I got back? Seven. Seven responses in total. Four of them were an unequivocal "no." I appreciated that they'd taken the time to reply at all, but the consolation lay in the fact that three of those responses held the promise of potential leads.

Then, just when I thought nothing would ever change, I received a call from a friend. She'd passed my pitch on to a potential investor—and he was interested. It felt too good to be true. Yet, I couldn't let myself get carried away. I couldn't afford to get my hopes up; disappointment had been a constant companion for too long. Almost immediately, the alarm bells began to ring in my mind. This investor wanted a payment of £3,500 before anything could move forward.

Seriously? I had been completely transparent in my emails and honest about my situation and what I was trying to build. People often say, "Don't show your weakness," and I get it. But surely, it's better to be honest and upfront? Here I was, being asked for £3,500—a sum I couldn't even fathom having, especially when my bank balance wouldn't even cover £3.50, let alone £3,500. After everything I'd been through—after all the struggle, all the pain—did he really think I had that kind of money to spare?

Of course, people like him didn't care about my circumstances. To them, it was just business—cold, calculated, and devoid of empathy. So, I turned to another business friend, someone who knew the ropes of this world far better than I did. She took it upon herself to call him, did some digging, and then came back with the truth: "This guy? He's not who he says he is."

Then, out of nowhere, she told me about another investor—a real one. A serious investor, with a huge fund, who only invested in projects over a million pounds. He was the

type who would actually look at both my magazine and my dating app. Over the years I had worked hard on the dating app and nearly 10 years later, the algorithms still worked. My passion to see people with fulfilling love and relationships stirred and better still, the prospect filled my heart with joy. I believed I could offer people true compatibility—and it worked. I'd been living it for years, guided by my ideas, my vision, and the long, painful road I'd walked to get here.

I sent him all the details—the story of the magazine, my vision, every hardship and every hope encapsulated in my pitch. I also sent the dating app pitch as they go hand in hand: the magazine serving as my free advertising. And as I sat there, staring at the sent email, my mind was a whirlwind of uncertainty. Was this it? Was this finally my chance to break through? I clung to that fragile hope, knowing that I wasn't giving up. I had come too far to turn back now.

He later confirmed that the investor was indeed in—finally, someone willing to help. We sent over all the documents, and more conversations followed. But then, every alarm bell in my head began ringing again: he wouldn't come on camera. That raised every possible red flag I had ever learned to recognise. Looking back now, I swear I would never accept anything from anyone unless I met them face-to-face or at the very least, had them on camera. If they're hiding something, there's usually a reason.

They sent over a bank statement to "prove" their legitimacy. I remember my initial reaction: I looked at it and gasped, "Bloody hell. Wowzers!" The statement reflected a balance of £916,442.00.

At first glance, it looked impressive, and I almost believed it until my instincts kicked in. After everything I had been through, trust . . . well, it had to be earned. I had been burned too many times to let my guard down now. I didn't trust them—not for a single moment. So, I did what anyone cautious would do: I checked it out.

I logged into my bank account and tried to make a £1 payment to test the numbers. Nothing matched; the figures just didn't add up. I then checked the other account they had provided—the supposed personal account of the investor—and red flags erupted. There was another account with a glaring red exclamation mark next to it, a signal that something was terribly amiss.

The truth began to unravel before my eyes. They weren't even based in the UK—they were operating out of the US. That revelation sent a chill down my spine, and I knew I had to dig deeper. I looked up the IBAN on iban.com, a site that promised legitimacy. It seemed to check out on the surface, but my gut, battered by years of disappointment, insisted something was off.

I printed the bank statement and studied it closely. My eyes zeroed in on the date—2023—but the transactions? They were all from 2022. And then I noticed the overdraft—just £16.00. Seriously? This investor was supposed to be sitting on nearly a million pounds, yet his overdraft was a mere £16. It simply didn't make any sense.

There it was then: the answer I didn't want to hear. It wasn't real.

I went back to square one, my heart heavy with the realisation that I couldn't keep chasing after false hope. The disappointments, the endless letdowns—they were too much to bear. Yet I couldn't let myself collapse either. I kept telling myself, "Don't be afraid to start over." Because this time, I wasn't starting from nothing—I was starting from experience, and that was worth so much more. Once bitten, twice shy, I reminded myself.

Weeks passed. Then months. And through it all, I kept grinding. More emails went out, more pitch decks were refined and sent, and countless sleepless nights piled on. I must've sent out hundreds of emails, most of which went unanswered. I couldn't stop, though—I had to keep going. I simply had to.

Then, out of the blue, another opportunity emerged—a glimmer of hope that made my heart race. But the universe, in its cruel irony, had other plans. The investor cancelled the day before our meeting. My heart sank so deep it felt as though it would never rise again. That meeting was supposed to be the breakthrough I'd been waiting for. I had scraped together every penny for the train fare—£24, a sum that, coupled with my exhaustion and despair, felt more like £20,000—and now it was all for nothing.

I cried. I felt as if I were perpetually one step away from something that could change everything, yet it always remained just out of reach. The weight of it all was utterly crushing. Every single day, I pushed through the exhaustion. Just yesterday, I had slogged through nearly 14 hours across two jobs. I was so drained that I could barely force myself to close my eyes at night. My body ached from the strain, and even as I went to bed, sleep eluded me.

Four hours later, I was up again, mechanically moving through the motions while every fibre of my being protested.

I took a long shower, desperately trying to wash away the persistent tiredness and the ache that clung to me like a second skin. But it didn't work. All I had left were sweat and tears, the only remnants of my dwindling energy. I cried again, but there was no time to wallow in self-pity. I had promises to keep and commitments to honour, and I wasn't about to let anyone down, no matter how much it hurt.

I had promised people I'd pay them back—even if it was just a few pounds—and I was determined to honour those promises, no matter how long it took, no matter how much it pained me. I couldn't keep putting it off; I couldn't keep running away from the reality of my obligations.

But, if I'm completely honest, I was at the edge. My body was screaming in protest. I was mentally and physically spent. Getting up at 5:30 a.m. and working until well past 8 or 10 p.m., barely scraping by, was draining every ounce of energy I had left. I had one day off, but even that day wasn't truly a day off. Even when I wasn't physically working, I was still working. I didn't have the luxury of shutting down; the bills didn't stop, the magazine didn't stop, and even in his late teens, my son's needs never really paused. Everything just kept going, relentlessly.

And sleep—oh, how I needed sleep. Yet it never came. I lay

there in the darkness, reflecting on my life and everything I had endured, wondering when it would all finally end.

Would it ever get better? Or was I destined to remain this worn out, barely surviving, dayafter endless day?

Every moment was a struggle, every minute a battle. Yet, amidst the chaos and heartache, I clung to a stubborn determination. I wasn't giving up. I was still fighting, still believing that someday, somehow, things would change. Because I had come too far to let false hope be the end of me. I was building something—even if it was one small piece at a time— toward a future where I could finally catch my breath. And maybe, just maybe, thatfuture would be worth every ounce of the pain and struggle along the way.

CHAPTER THIRTEEN:

The Breakdown

In the meantime, my whole world was falling apart—I was utterly skint, so broke that I was forced to deposit a cheque at the post office—a service some UK banks offer through postal branches—just to save on petrol and parking. It was a small, desperate act, a final grasp at survival that somehow seemed to be my only option. But then, just a week later—when I was promised only two days' grace—my bank informed me they hadn't received it. I checked my account and saw it: 48p. That's all I had left. Forty-eight pence. The remaining petrol in my car which was my mum's car would barely get me 30 miles, and I desperately needed to get to work in the morning. And then, as if that wasn't enough, the cheque came back.

I had to fill out a form and take it to the bank in person. I drove to town, parked my car with barely any money for parking, and trudged inside, my heart pounding with anxiety and humiliation. When I arrived, I couldn't believe my eyes: workmen were inside, and the bank was closed for refurbishment. They told me I needed to go to another branch, 30 minutes away—and I didn't have enough petrol for that journey. At that moment, I just broke down. I couldn't hold it together any longer.

How could life keep pushing me like this? Why is it so FUCKING HARD? I couldn't take it anymore—emotionally, physically, mentally drained to the point of collapse. Every part of me was exhausted, and the weight of it all was suffocating.

I broke down.

I couldn't hold it together any longer. How could life keep pushing me like this? Why is it so FUCKING HARD? I wasn't just tired—I was annihilated.

Emotionally, physically, mentally wrecked. My insides felt hollow, scraped raw. Like I was drowning in stone—heavy, slow, sinking under pressure that never let up.

Every breath felt like dragging air through broken glass. Every thought was a fog I couldn't clear.

I was suffocating in plain sight.

And yet—I had a business call in 30 minutes. I was supposed to sit upright, smile, sound capable and pretend I hadn't just crumbled into myself minutes before.

I couldn't keep doing this.

This endless charade of "I'm fine."

I wasn't fine. I wasn't even functional.

I didn't know where to turn. I couldn't even afford the stamp to send the chequeback—a stamp. That tiny, ridiculous symbol of how far I'd fallen.

I had nothing left.

Not pride. Not energy. Not options. Just the crushing silence of holding myself together in a world that never stopped asking for more.

I had a business call in just 30 minutes, and I was expected to pull myself together, to pretend nothing was wrong. I couldn't keep up this endless charade. I didn't know where to turn; I couldn't even afford the stamp to send the cheque back. I had nothing left.

The brutal reality hit like a freight train: I wasn't built for a typical 9-to-5 grind. And yet, I was working from 5:30 a.m. on some mornings until 10 p.m., barely scraping by. I had a purpose, I knew it deep down—I wanted to help people, to inspire them with my work. But right now, at this moment, I needed to find a way to help myself first. I needed to survive.

Sitting in my car, feeling as if the entire world was collapsing around me, I thought about everything I had endured and how far I had come, yet how much further I still had to go. My head was spinning, my heart aching with despair, and I wondered if I could really keep fighting.

My pain would build something—it had to.

I reflected on how much I had changed over the years. If I had gotten that TV show a few years ago, I don't think I'd be the person I am now. I wouldn't have learned, grown, or been shaped by these relentless challenges. I thought of that Emma Thompson quote: "It's unfortunate, and I really wish I wouldn't have to say this, but I really like human beings who have suffered. They're kinder." It's a heartbreaking truth, but one which resonates with me. I realised then, that there is purpose in pain—if only we could be kind to ourselves.

It's funny how life works. You spend years chasing work, money, and status, convinced that these are the things that matter. But when you listen to people on their deathbeds, they're not asking for cars, degrees, or even businesses. They just want family, friends, and love. While I continued to reflect, the sentiment stopped me in my tracks. All the work I was doing—what was it really for? Was it worth sacrificing the most important things in life if I lost the very essence of what makes me human?

I thought about my dad—how he'd watched his own father struggle with bills, how that drove him to work harder than anyone I knew. But at what cost? His life was all about the grind, the endless pursuit of money. Even when he succeeded, he never let go of that mindset. And I, too, had adopted that same relentless drive. Yet, looking back now, I see that success isn't measured solely in money—it's about love, relationships, and the connections we forge. I wondered if my dad ever regretted not letting love in sooner or if he ever longed for a little warmth beyond the constant pressure to earn.

I realised how much I'd been chasing: proving myself, building something from nothing, and accumulating success by any means necessary. Perhaps this was the moment I was meant to slow down and see that there's more to life than the endless grind. I cried while typing these words, wishing he had let love in, and realising I needed to learn that too. Life isn't just about grinding away; it's about cherishing the people we love and who love us in return. It's about living with no regrets.

On my birthday—a day that should be filled with celebration, I couldn't stop the tears. Another year had passed, and I still wasn't where I wanted to be. Yet, deep inside, I knew that maybe I was exactly where I was meant to be. I have nothing, but I'm still breathing. And that, in itself, is something.

Amidst the crushing despair and the weight of endless struggle, I knew I had to keep fighting. I was on the edge, yes—but if I could make it through this darkness, then maybe, just maybe, there would be light at the end of the tunnel. And that, above all, makes every tear, every sleepless night, and every aching moment, worth it.

Then, my son, made my day. He blew up balloons and decorated the room with such simple, beautiful joy. It made me feel so much better and so grateful. It reminded me that life isn't about money or expensive gifts—it's about the time and effort you give and the love you share. Those small gestures filled my heart. I'd even received some good news.

One dreary afternoon, I received a phone call from the courts. My heart pounded so fiercely that I thought it might burst from my chest. This time, though, the news was entirely different. Damien had pleaded guilty. At that moment, I felt a weight lift off my shoulders—I didn't have to go to court. I didn't have to fight this battle anymore. There was a profound relief, not just for me, but, strangely enough, for him as well. I clung to a fragile hope that this was his turning point, that he might finally learn from his mistakes and begin living a life unburdened by his past transgressions. With sentencing scheduled for December, there was at least some semblance of closure. It wasn't the happy ending I had imagined, but it was the relief I desperately needed.

In the quiet aftermath of that call, I sat alone and let the silence envelop me. I realised that while things were far from perfect, the struggle and the pain had begun to carve out space for growth. In those rare, peaceful moments, when all the chaos subsided, I started to see glimmers of light at the end of the tunnel. I wondered if this was the moment when everything might finally begin to turn around.

Then, out of the blue, a few months later, my phone rang again. This time, it was a TV executive with the same first name as me—Lisa! "Would you be free to meet up?" she asked. "I'm looking at a TV show and want to speak to you." On one hand, I felt a spark of excitement—a tiny flame of possibility in the darkness. On the other hand, I was utterly knackered. My bank balance was a dismal -£18.18, and my body felt utterly wrecked and tired. Did I have the energy to relive every heartbreak and hardship all over again? But deepdown, I knew I had to try. This could be the break I'd been waiting for—a chance to pay offall my debts and maybe even treat myself to a week on a beach, doing absolutely nothing. I wasn't sure I'd ever be able to move on from the grind if I stopped now.

So, I did what I had to do. I borrowed some money, put my head down, and got backon the grind—because in my world, you have to put on a brave face. If I went into that meeting and showed them how I was really feeling—a tired soul who didn't even want to talk—I knew I wouldn't get anywhere. So, I summoned every bit of courage I had and put ona show. It was a bit like going back to school, when I'd felt sad on the inside and had to wear a brave face on the outside and be funny and engaging—something I had grown all too accustomed to. And I did just that.

As the meeting unfolded, something unexpected happened. I reached a point where I didn't care about pretence anymore—I was just me, in a purer, happier form of myself. The version of me that could smile despite everything, that had that spark of hope which was fuelled by dreams of a holiday on a sunny beach, even if only for a little while. The executivesaid they would be in touch, and as I left, a weight I'd carried for so long began to lift. I realised that at this stage in my life, I no longer expected anything. If opportunities arose, they were meant to be; if they didn't, then perhaps they weren't meant for me. That's the wayI now look at life—one moment at a time, with no grand expectations.

The truth had begun to set in: I had reached a stage in my life where I no longer clungdesperately to every promise of change. I had learned to accept that life could be a series of unpredictable turns—if something was meant to be, it would happen. And if not, then that was simply part of the journey.

I had endured so much that setbacks no longer surprised me; they were merelyanother part of my story.

As I drove home that day, my mind was a jumbled mix of exhaustion and cautious optimism. I thought back over everything—every sleepless night, every rejection, every crushing disappointment—and yet, here I was, still fighting. I recalled how, even when my bank balance was in the red and my body ached from the constant grind, I kept pushing forward. I was determined to keep building something, brick by brick, moment by moment.

The TV show invitation, though unexpected, was a sign that perhaps my efforts were finallypaying off.

I reflected on how far I had come: from a time when I could barely scrape together a few pennies to get by, to this moment when an opportunity, however tentative, might finally allow me to lift myself out of the endless cycle of hardship. It wasn't just about the money orthe fame; it was about proving to myself that I was capable of more, and that I had the resilience to endure even the darkest days.

In that long, introspective drive, I began to understand that my journey was not defined solely by my hardships, but also by my capacity to rise above them. Every call, every pitch, every heart-wrenching setback had contributed to shaping a stronger, more determined version of myself. I was learning that sometimes, the light at the end of the tunnel isn't a beacon of immediate salvation, but a slow, steady glow that grows brighter with each step forward.

Yes, life had knocked me down countless times, but I was, still standing. And as I made my way home, the possibility of a better future, however uncertain, filled me with a quiet determination. I resolved to keep fighting, to keep believing that every setback was just a prelude to a new beginning—when I could finally have the life, I'd dreamed of having, even if it took every last ounce of strength I had.

CHAPTER FOURTEEN:

From Stuffing Doughnuts to Meeting the Royal Family

My life was nothing short of chaotic—sometimes I wondered how I managed to keep it all together. I was up at 5 a.m., dragging myself out of bed to head to my new job at a bakery, where I spent my day stuffing doughnuts. The hours were early, the work was physically demanding, and even though it was different from my cleaning job, it was still gruelling in its own way. There were moments I could have collapsed from exhaustion, especially when I barely had enough petrol in the tank to even get there.

But then, one day everything changed. It was a big day—a day that promised magic amidst the madness. I needed to get into London for a meeting, yet I faced the impossible: almost no petrol, a near-empty bank balance, and the constant gnaw of hunger.

At home, there'd been scarcely anything to eat—just a few jacket potatoes that, if rationed properly, might stretch for four days. In desperate bids to make ends meet, I often scraped together 20p for a loaf of bread—enough, combined with a generous spread of Marmite, to cover my lunches for a week. This was my life: scraping by, battling hunger and exhaustion, yet still chasing glimmers of possibility.

And then, in the midst of all the chaos, I was about to meet one of the members of the royal family. Royalty. It seemed so surreal. There I was, juggling cleaning and baking, suddenly on the brink of entering a world so polished and refined it might as well have been another universe. My son, bless his heart, had lent me money for the train fare. Without him, I honestly don't know how I would've managed to get there. Nerves churned in my stomach like a turbulent sea.

I had to keep reminding myself that this was a chance—a colossal, life-changing opportunity. Even though I felt like Cinderella on the verge of an overwhelming transformation, my reality had been built from grit, exhaustion, and endless struggle. This meeting could be the key: perhaps it would bring a member of the royal family to grace our magazine's front cover, or better yet, to write for us. That would not only boost our profile but could even help attract investors. In the background, I still had potential breakthroughs—a TV show possibility and a dating app project that I'd nurtured for years, each representing a fragment of my shattered yet persistent dreams. For over twelve years, I had worked seven days a week, nearly 12 hours a day, driven by a burning desire for security, stability, and yes, even for a bloody holiday—an escape to a sunlit beach where I could finally let go of everything.

Today, however, I had to stay focused. As I got ready, my nerves were fraying at the edges. I questioned whether I was overdressed; the nice dress I'd chosen felt almost too extravagant in the morning's chill. I could feel sweat beading on my forehead as I adjusted my outfit, but there was no time for second-guessing. I straightened my shoulders, summoned the best version of myself, and vowed to simply be me—authentic and unyielding.

And then, of course, the rain hit. Typical British weather—the clouds opened up, drenching everything in a silvery downpour. My hair frizzed wildly, and I couldn't help butlaugh at the absurdity of it all. I looked a bit like Tina Turner. Although Tina's hair looked amazing on her, it looked ridiculous on me—I lacked her effortless glamour. Still, I held onto that laugh as a defiant act, a reminder that I had made it this far, no matter how ridiculous I might appear.

Arriving at the private members' club in London was like stepping into a different dimension. Everything was polished, every surface gleaming under warm lights, and the atmosphere hummed with quiet sophistication. But when I finally met him—the member of the royal family who had agreed to speak with me—all my nerves seemed to melt away. He was kind and approachable, exuding a warmth that made it easy to forget the daunting surroundings.

We spoke about the magazine, and I poured out my vision with all the passion and exhaustion that had defined my journey. He listened intently, his eyes twinkling with genuine interest. Despite the formality of the setting, he carried himself with a refreshing lack of pretension. He confided that he hated having his photo taken, and thus wouldn't be on the cover, but he was more than open to writing for us. That was monumental—a member of the royal family offering his words to our project, drawn to its profile, could change everything.

As we continued our conversation, he even offered to introduce me to others who could help bring our cause to life. When it came time to pay for our drinks, I fretted quietly about the cost, knowing every penny mattered. To my surprise, he insisted on covering the bill—a small act of chivalry that felt almost magical given everything I had been through.

That moment was transformative. It wasn't just a meeting—it was a turning point.

The chaos of my life, the ceaseless grinding of daily survival, all seemed to coalesce into this singular instance of hope. For the first time in ages, I could envision a future where the endless struggle might finally yield something beautiful. Even as I navigated a world of scant resources, fierce determination, and unyielding hardship, here was a beacon of possibility that shone through like a ray of sunlight breaking through storm clouds.

In that sparkling moment of contrast—between the grime of early mornings and the polished elegance of a London club—I realised that life, as chaotic and brutal as it sometimes was, held moments of magic. Magic in the kindness of strangers, in the unexpected opportunities that emerged when you least anticipated them, and in the quiet strength of a heart that refuses to give up.

I left that meeting with a head swirling with ideas, my battered soul momentarily lifted by the encounter. I knew that the road ahead would be steep and fraught with challenges, but that one shimmering conversation had rekindled my belief that every hardship, every sleepless night and tearful morning, had been leading me towards something extraordinary.

And so, even as I continued to juggle cleaning floors, stuffing doughnuts, and chasing my dreams with every fibre of my being, I held onto that spark of magic. I knew that one day, the relentless grind might give way to a life filled with more than just survival—a life rich with hope, love, and the sweet taste of victory. Today, I choose to believe that despite the chaos, despite the endless struggle, there is beauty waiting at the end of the tunnel. And thatbelief, fragile though it may be, is what keeps me moving forward, one determined step at atime.

I left the meeting feeling like something real was happening. Sure, it wasn't a monumental win yet, but the potential was undeniable: a small step forward—a giant leap in my world, where every tiny victory mattered. There I was, a woman who spent her days scrubbing floors and stuffing doughnuts, and yet I had just experienced a once-in-a-lifetime moment—someone huge believed in me and my magazine! In my reality, it was nothing shortof a breakthrough. Perhaps—just perhaps—this was the break I'd been working so relentlessly to achieve.

But as the day drew to a close, reality came crashing back. Tomorrow meant returning to the bakery, back to the grind of doughnuts and early mornings. I couldn't help but wonder: when would it all end? Would I ever escape the clutches of the bakery and step into something greater—a life that offered the financial stability I'd long dreamed of? As much as I hoped for that transformation, the future still felt uncertain and precarious.

Still, I couldn't allow myself to slow down. I continued sending emails to investors—hundreds of them, sometimes— refusing to give up, even when fatigue and discouragement threatened to overtake me. Every pitch, every desperate email was a testament to my refusal to quit. The magazine needed more funding to grow and to reach the people who needed to see the stories we were telling. Juggling the magazine, securing investors for the dating app or the magazine while managing my day-to-day jobs to pay the bills was overwhelming, but I had no choice. I had to keep pushing forward.

Then, something incredible happened: an email from Serena Williams's company.

Yes, Serena Williams. They had reached out, expressing genuine interest in our magazine and requested more information. That tiny glimmer of hope was electrifying—a well-earned victory, however small. I clutched onto that feeling tightly—more proof that all my hard work was starting to pay off.

Yet even as hope bloomed, life continued to throw challenges my way. I still had to make those gut-wrenching decisions. For instance, should I buy new work trousers? The ones I had were falling apart—a gaping hole in the crotch that seemed to widen with each wear. It wasn't ideal, but what choice did I have? Every penny mattered. I had to decide whether to spend my meagre funds on a new pair of trousers or invest it into the magazine, my future. Of course, I chose the magazine. The trousers were just trousers, but the magazine was the lifeline I had been building with every desperate, hopeful breath.

A few months passed, and slowly things began to turn around. I had spent nearly a year perfecting the magazine as it was going up against Vogue and Harrods magazines. I was under pressure to meet impossibly high standards—but could I, the kid on the special bus, really pull it off? Well, F**k me! I did it! I received approval to distribute our magazine in 600 luxury locations around the world. People were beginning to take notice.

What had started as a hobby became more than a pastime— it'd become my lifeline, now evolving into a bona fide business—and growing. The excitement was palpable. I remembered the countless hours spent perfecting every detail, printing new copies over and over, even when I had to dip into what little I had for food money. Each print run was a labour of love, and every time I saw the final product, I couldn't help but feel a surge of pride. It looked fantastic—like the absolute dog's bollocks, as we used to say—and I was so proud that I'd managed to create something out of nothing.

Yet, I still needed more—a sales team, more investors, and sufficient funding to scale up the business. Without the money, I knew I wouldn't be able to build it further. I wasn't there yet, but I was closer than ever before. I could feel the momentum growing, a tide lifting all my hard-won progress. No matter how tired I felt, no matter how many setbacks came my way, I knew I was on the right path.

Perhaps things were finally beginning to shift. It had taken a tremendous amount of hard work, sacrifices, and moments of soul-crushing doubt, but here I was, still standing and still fighting. I wasn't giving up—not now, not when I could see the future starting to take shape before my eyes.

And just like that, my life transformed—from days spent stuffing doughnuts to the surreal experience of meeting royalty and obscurity to moments of genuine opportunity. If that's not a sign that anything can happen, then I don't know what is. I clung to that belief, nurturing it with every small victory and bit of progress, as I continued on my unpredictable, magical journey toward a better life.

CHAPTER FIFTEEN:

Where Am I Today?

It's funny when I look back on my life. It all began with school and that deep-seated fear that I was never good enough—never clever enough, never intelligent enough. I still remember the day I was told I'd have to take the "special bus." That label, that constant reminder that I was different, left an indelible mark on my young mind. I let others dictate my narrative for far too long, allowing their harsh words and dismissive actions to write the early chapters of my life. Those feelings of inadequacy and fear seeped into every fibre of my being and clung to me as I moved through the phases.

For so long, I found myself chasing the approval of everyone around me. I yearned for my father's approval, desperately trying to win his praise even though his love was expressed only through silence and hard work. I longed for the love of John—the kind of love I thought would fill the emptiness inside me, but what I didn't realise, was that a seed must be destroyed before it can bloom—sometimes, things must fall apart before they can begin anew.

This book is more than a memoir—it's a record of hitting rock bottom, survival, healing, and finally stepping into a voice I wasn't sure I was ever meant to have.

I didn't just rebuild a business—I rebuilt myself.

And that took more than grit. It took unlearning the belief that I wasn't enough, that I didn't belong, and that I didn't deserve to be heard.

Writing this book as someone with dyslexia was its own mountain. Every sentence you read here has been wrestled into place—words slipping off the page, forcing me to drag them back again and again. Emails that took hours. Paragraphs that read like puzzles. But I pushed. And pushed. And pushed. Because I knew my story mattered, even if I'd spent most of my life believing it didn't.

At the time, I couldn't understand the role Damien played in my life. His presence was stormy and complicated. But looking back, I see now—he was part of the lesson. His influence marked me in ways that made me look at what I accepted and why.

In my twenties, I used alcohol not to lose control, but to gain it. I wasn't an alcoholic in the traditional sense—but I leaned on it as a crutch. It gave me just enough false confidence to survive a world that constantly told me I wasn't enough. It numbed the ache of unhealed wounds, if only for a while.

Those early years—the bullying, the special bus, the labels: dunce, div, spaz—and all the traumas left scars that took years to uncover and even longer to heal. I wasn't writing my own story back then. I was reacting to pain, to survival, to fear. I let others define me until I finally decided no more.

This book is my truth. It's messy, painful, hopeful, and real.

If you see yourself in these pages—know this: You can survive, too.

You can rebuild.

You can rise.

Even if the words fall off the page, you can still write a story worth telling.

When I finally began to heal, that's when I started writing my own chapter, forging a path that was uniquely mine. I remember the moment I truly listened to my inner voice—a quiet, persistent whisper that had been drowned out by years of noise and distraction. I finallyunderstood that my calling was to inspire others, to give hope, and to share stories that uplift the spirit. And that was when the idea for the magazine was born.

I envisioned the magazine as so much more than a collection of articles. I wanted it to be a sanctuary—a space that covered everything from health and wellbeing to business, finance, fashion, and homes. I dreamed of a publication that was both an enjoyable escape and a meaningful source of inspiration, one that would leave a lasting impact on its readers' lives. To achieve that, I sought out the best experts and thought leaders, those who could share their wisdom and insights with sincerity and compassion. I wanted the magazine to answer the questions that many of us have, to provide the guidance we desperately seek, and to warm our hearts with stories of resilience and perseverance.

I found inspiration in the journeys of people like John, in John's Crazy Socks and Atul.

John, who was born with Down syndrome, refused to let his condition define him.

Alongside his father, he transformed his love for colourful socks into a thriving business. His venture became much more than a company; it spread joy, provided employment opportunities for people with disabilities, and supported charitable causes. It was a testament to what passion and determination could achieve when one refused to be limited by circumstance.

Similarly, Atul, who was born with cerebral palsy, built a successful event business from scratch. When the pandemic forced his business to halt, he didn't give up; instead, he pivoted and launched Atul Skincare. Using family recipes, he created a range of chemical-free skincare products. His philosophy— "You can have reasons or results, but reasons don't count"—became his mantra, inspiring him to push past obstacles and encouraging others to do the same.

Their stories of overcoming pain, heartbreak, and adversity resonated deeply with me. They were living proof that hope and determination can rewrite any story, no matter how dark the beginning. These journeys reaffirmed why I created the magazine—to inspire, uplift, and remind people that even in our most vulnerable moments, we have the power to rise again.

When you put the magazine down, you won't just feel inspired—you'll feel empowered. That's what makes Mind Jump Magazine truly different.

I realised that the lessons I had once internalised—the fear of not being enough, the relentless chase for approval—could be transformed into fuel for change. I began to see that my past, with all its scars, had equipped me with the empathy and strength needed to create something truly special. I started to write my own story, not as a victim, but as a survivor with a message. The magazine became my way of turning pain into purpose, of sharing the raw, unfiltered truth of life with those who might need it most.

Now, as I look back on those early, painful years, I understand that every moment of struggle was a stepping stone to this very moment of creation. I have learned that the value of life is not measured by the approval of others, but by the courage to follow your own path, to transform your wounds into wisdom. In doing so, I hope to inspire others to do the same—to believe that even when the world tells you you're not enough, you can rise, you can create, and you can shine.

And now, here we are—at a point where my life has taken a turn I could never have imagined. Where am I today? It's an exciting new chapter. We've been approved to distribute our magazine in over 600 prestigious venues around the globe. Imagine that: my publication gracing the walls of airports like Gatwick and Heathrow, adorning the lobbies of iconic hotels such as The Ritz, The Savoy, and the Waldorf Astoria, and making its mark in places as illustrious as Beverly Hills, Paris, Monte Carlo, Dubai, and many more. We've reached the most exclusive hotels, spas, golf clubs, airports, and private members' clubs—a dream that once seemed as distant as the stars.

But beyond the glittering locations and impressive numbers, I want this journey to be a message for anyone who has ever felt "not enough." I want you to believe in yourself. If I—the kid who was labelled "stupid" and forced onto the "special bus"—if I, someone who endured turmoil, lost two homes, had no car, no food, and yet managed to create something from nothing, then you can do it too. I had no money, no advantages, but I had sheer determination. I built a dating app, pitched a TV show, and created a magazine—things I had never done before. I learned the art of writing and reading, and I discovered that my greatest weakness could be turned into my superpower.

Do you remember when I first started the dating app in that

tiny caravan? I was driven by one simple desire—to help people find love and happiness. For years, I dedicated myself to matchmaking, but I wasn't always sure what the end goal was. Yes, I wanted to help people, and yes, the TV show was part of that journey. But why?

It's funny when I look back. I had this dream of creating a dating app, and deep down, I knew the magazine would help—it was free advertising, after all. But the app itself? After spending nearly 12 years perfecting the algorithm and refining every detail to ensure it could truly connect people in a meaningful way, I almost walked away from it all.

Then it hit me. I couldn't let those years of work, of learning, of love just go to waste.

I had something special, something that no one else had—years of real matchmaking experience, distilled into an algorithm that could actually change lives. And in the process of helping others find love, I finally found it in myself.

It's ironic, really. The moment I truly embraced self-love, everything started to fall into place. Do you remember when I talked about how a seed has to be destroyed before it can bloom? —that sometimes, things fall apart before something new can begin? That moment didn't come at the start of this chapter—it came right here. This was my breaking point and my turning point. I had to let go of the old version of me—the one who doubted, hesitated, and second-guessed everything—to become who I was truly meant to be.

(Only wish it hadn't taken this f**king long, lol.)

I changed my life by healing myself, by believing in myself. I stopped drinking and started eating properly; I haven't had a drink for over two years now, and I don't miss it.

A friend once joked, "What if you ever get married again? Would you have a glass ofchampagne to celebrate?"

I laughed. Well, yes, I probably would have a drink then!

But Me? Marry again? I love myself too much now. If I ever did find someone to share my life with, they would have to be truly special—but I no longer need someone else tocomplete me. I have completely turned my life around—I've come full circle, and I've never felt more content.

Yet, I still carried one weight—the pain of the dating app stalling. Hadn't I done enough already? Although the magazine was my baby, and I knew it was helping people,deep down, I also knew I had to finish the dating app. I couldn't let more people suffer through painful, toxic relationships. I knew matchmaking wasn't sustainable—too much time, too much energy. But the app? That could scale. That could reach millions.

So, I built a team. Experts. People who believed in the vision I had been "birthing" foryears. I went out and pitched to people and companies—and one of the UK's biggest firms loved it. They even said they'd back the second round.

Bloody hell! The first round is always the hardest, but we weren't asking for millions—just over £200K. I'd already built TV ads and spent two years mapping out how to make them land emotionally. I needed something that would go viral. And this will sound a bit woo-woo, but I had a dream—weeks of thinking, praying—and then I saw it. Clear as day. A vision, a message from God, showing me exactly how this would take off. Disruptive.

Powerful. Viral.

I knew I had everything I needed. I just needed the money.

Well, let's just see what happens. Because I know in my heart that I was put on this earth to help people. The magazine will give people insight, inspiration, and space to breathe.

But the dating app? That could give people something even deeper—real love, truecompatibility, connection.

That's what I believe in. That's why I keep going.

I changed my life by healing myself—by finally believing in myself.

I still work hard, and I genuinely enjoy my work because I know that every day bringsa new opportunity.

My son, my health, and the abundance of happiness and love in my life remind methat I am exactly where I'm meant to be.

So, don't listen to the naysayers; don't let the doubts of others hold you back. If you have a dream, dream big. And then, do something about it. You have the power to write your own story, to shape your own future. I don't want anyone to lie on their deathbed with regrets. I've spoken to many elderly people, and one of their biggest regrets is not spending enough time with loved ones, not pursuing their passions, and not being true to themselves.

They regret not taking risks, not expressing their feelings, and, most painfully, not beinghappier.

Don't let fear control you. Take back control. Write your next chapter. I've found that many older individuals wish they had been braver, that they had taken more chances. They were so afraid to fail that they never even tried. I too, have had moments of fear. There were times when I hesitated and when I didn't act.

But if I had been braver, I might have started my business much sooner. It doesn't matter when you start—what matters is that you take that first step. It's never too late to begin.

I still can't believe the stupid kid, who wasn't stupid at all, has her magazine in TheSavoy, The Ritz and nearly every airport across the world. That image is not just a snapshotof where I am today, but a symbol of how far I've come—and how far you too can go. I've achieved my dream. I wanted my magazine to be more than just a publication; it's a collection of beautiful stories that spread joy, knowledge, and hope. It isn't about fear-mongering or scaring people; it's about offering warmth, insights, and upliftingnarratives that can change lives.

So, wherever you are today, know that it's never too late to start writing your next chapter. It doesn't matter what has happened in your past or how many obstacles you've faced. What matters is that you decide, today, to take control of your life—to believe in yourself and to keep moving forward. That's how you create a life you're proud of. And whoknows? Maybe your story will inspire someone else to do the same.

I can bravely say today, as I sit with my tiara firmly on my head, that I am here, and Iam ready. Ready to embrace the future, to inspire others, and to show that if I can make it from a life of chaos and hardship to one filled with opportunities and hope, then anyone can.

Dream big, my friends, and never stop writing your own story. And in case you werewondering—that beach vacation I'd been longing for is finally within reach.

Reflections and Understanding

"A seed has to be destroyed before it can bloom."
- Lisa Holley Palmer

I wanted validation—for people to like me, to love me. The truth is, I didn't truly love myself, yet I longed for everyone else to love me. When I entered this world, I did so through the energy of not being loved, of not being wanted. And as they say, you always crave what you don't have. For me, that illusive thing was love.

As such, Mind Jump magazine is full of love and stories—woven with struggle and triumph—about people who deeply resonated with me and reaffirmed the very reason I created the magazine: to inspire, uplift, and remind others that our pasts don't define our futures. Readers might find something in the magazine that uplifts them while also warming their hearts with powerful stories of love, connection, and resilience.

One of the most difficult stories I endured was the complicated relationship I had with my dad. The way he showed his love wasn't through touch, affection, or words. He only knew one way to show love—to provide a roof over our heads and food on the table. As a child, I didn't understand it. It was hard. But today, I do. So, if you have a relationship in your life—perhaps with your dad, husband, boyfriend, or grandad—that you struggle to understand, take a step back. Try to see things from their perspective. Ask yourself: what happened to them? Why are they the way they are?

It's funny that so much of life is about patterns. We follow them without even realising. For example, my nan would always put a piece of meat in a tin to cook it, having cut the ends off every single time. Then my mum did the same. I never understood why. One day, I asked her, and she said she did it because my nan did. Then I asked my nan why she did it, and it turned out it was simply because the meat wouldn't fit in her little tin! That's how it works—we follow patterns, habits, and behaviours passed down to us.

My dad is no different. I once told you the story of when he saw my grandad break down in tears because he had no money. From that moment, my dad swore he would never be in that position. That's why he worked so hard, grafting day and night. And I am so proud of what he achieved. No one gave him anything—he earned every bit of it. I joke with him, calling him a tight git, but would I have changed him? No. Because if he had done things differently, I wouldn't be who I am today.

If he had helped me financially, I wouldn't have stood on my own two feet. It was hard, don't get me wrong—it wasn't easy. But if he had made things easier for me, I never would have healed, grown, or learned to be independent. I would have always leaned on someone else to look after me. I had to learn to stand on my own.

Relationships are hard, but they shape us. However, never let people control you.

That's why it is 100% important to have your own bank account, stand on your own two feet, be proud of who you are, and do what you want. Don't listen to others. And I don't mean be reckless—what I mean to say is if you want to be a singer, lawyer, dog breeder—do it. Listen to your soul. Don't leave this earth with regrets.

Do you remember when I was living in the caravan, working on the dating site, and spending all those years matchmaking? Some people might have looked at my relationships and asked, "How can she help others when her own relationships aren't perfect?" And to that, I say—yes, I agree. But those experiences, both the beautiful moments and the painful lessons, had taught me more than I could have ever imagined.

It's easy to recognise red flags when you're looking out for someone else—when there are no emotions involved. But when it's *your* heart on the line, that's when it becomes difficult. I spent years developing algorithms to help people find their right match, but after a decade of doing this, I realised something profound: the best insights come from those who have walked through the fire. Who better to understand love than someone who has endured heartbreak, loss, and growth? I wouldn't wish the pain I went through on anyone, and that's exactly why I created something to help others avoid it.

Would I go back and relive it all again? No. It was incredibly hard. But would I change anything? Also no. Because every lesson, every tear, and every setback was part of my destiny. That's why I knew I had to finish what I started in that caravan. When I first built the dating app, it was like all the others—just another platform for people to meet. But that wasn't enough. I didn't just want people to *find* love—I wanted them to find *true*, fulfilling love.

Love isn't about what you get. It's about partnership. It's about support, someone wanting you to be the best version of you. Think about it—maybe you're a dog breeder, and you're exhausted from waking up at all hours to feed the puppies. Maybe you're a parent, overwhelmed and trying to juggle it all. Love is having a partner who sees you struggling and steps in to help—not because they have to, but because they *want* to. Maybe they take over a night feed so you can sleep. Maybe they cook you a meal so you can put your feet up for once. That's love. Lifting each other up. Being happy for one another. Supporting each other through life's chaos.

Finding someone who truly fits your heart's needs—your *XYZ*—isn't easy. That's why I created the app. I never want anyone to go through the kind of pain I went through, and when I sat in that caravan, I vowed to build the *best* dating platform in the world—one that actually helps people find deep, meaningful love.

The first two years were spent just putting the app together, but it wasn't enough.

Matchmaking, life coaching, relationship coaching, and my training as a Reiki master have all helped me understand people more deeply and broadly. And now, with every facet of my healing and self-discovery having shaped my understanding, the app is finished.

I'm out for investment, and maybe by the time you read this, the app will be live. If not, let's pray that someone sees the vision and helps me bring it to life—because with all my heart, I want to help people find love.

It's funny—there was one final piece of the jigsaw that I needed before completing the app. I had all the algorithms and all the systems in place, but something was missing. I asked God and my angels to help me, knowing deep down they would. And then I waited. Nothing happened, so I completely surrendered, trusting the answer would come when thetime was right.

Then, a week later, I had a dream. *They* showed me the missing piece—the final partof the puzzle for my dating app. And at that moment, I knew I was ready. Perhaps my whole destiny was leading me here—to create something that would bring *real* love to humanity.

I felt it. That same warmth in my heart, the same *knowing* I had when I created the magazine—my soul coming alive because it knows I've built something powerful, somethinglife-changing.

Now, here I go again—searching for an investor. It's exhausting, but I know God will help me with this too. In the meantime, keep your eye out for the app—it's called **Goddess**.

Why *Goddess*? Because it's after Aphrodite, the Greek Goddess of Love. And that's exactly what this app is about— bringing true, deep, meaningful love into people's lives.

I do think back to my ex, John, and I truly wish him well. I hope he works on his issues and becomes the good man I know he was meant to be. I remember how he both lovedand hated the attention I received, driven by his own insecurities. I allowed him to treat me poorly for far too long, yet I learned that sometimes love is as complicated as it is painful.

I've grown apart from him, and while anger and regret once festered within me, I have since come to understand that every relationship, even the ones that hurt, teach invaluable lessons. I only have love in my heart for John because he will always be a part of me and one of the reasons, I am who I am today. How could I not love that?

Reflecting on my past also drudges up memories of Damien—his attention, his moments of kindness mixed with cruelty. I craved the validation he provided because, in his own twisted way, he did make me feel special. He was my drug, my kryptonite. His presence was a volatile mix of bliss and torment, and while I once blamed him for my pain, I now see him as a wounded soul dealing with his own trauma. He too, taught me about the complexities of love and the importance of healing.

I remember the day I received an eviction notice, a moment flooded with anxiety, shame, and a crushing sense of failure—terrified of dragging my son through another ordeal. Owing money and constantly struggling to stay afloat contributed to feeling physically ill.

There were nights when I sat alone in the dark, tears streaming down my face, questioning whether I could ever escape this cycle of despair. But I kept going. I kept working and kept fighting, and somehow, I grew stronger and more resilient with each passing day.

I still remember standing in the benefits office, a place I never thought I'd find myself. I broke down in tears there, feeling utterly humiliated and emotionally shattered. But even in that vulnerability, I found a strange sort of grace. The man at the office, kind and empathetic, handed me tissues and told me that it was refreshing to see someone who genuinely cared—someone who cared, even if they felt like a failure. At that moment, I began to understand that every obstacle, every moment of despair, was part of a greater journey—one that was meant to break me down only to build me back up again.

A seed has to be destroyed before it can bloom!

Looking back now, it's almost surreal to see how far I've come. I can see how weak I once was, how I was consumed by my fear of confrontation, and how desperately I sought validation from others. Today, I understand that those trials were necessary. I believe that before coming into this world, I agreed to face these obstacles, knowing that they would forge a resilience within me that would carry me forward. I have learned to support and love myself, and in doing so, I have discovered that the love I once desperately sought from otherswas within me all along.

So, here I stand today—bruised, scarred, but undeniably stronger. I've written my own story, and I hope that by sharing it, others who feel "not enough" can see that they, too, have the power to bloom. No matter how dark the past is, there is always a future waiting tobe written—a future filled with hope, love, and endless possibilities.

And I did. I am strong now. Strangely, I've come to be grateful for the hardships—because today, I love the person I've become. She's the best version of me. I amkind, yet I no longer tolerate bad manners or allow negativity to seep into my life. I had to raise my vibration to match the person I wanted to be. I still see goodness in people, I remainkind, but I listen to my gut now.

When I reflect on my past, I see it clearly: I was living at a very low vibration. I didn'tlove myself; I didn't respect myself, and I had no boundaries. I was too nice, too accepting, letting the world trample over me. But that girl is gone now. Today, I won't allow that to happen again—I respect myself far too much. If you feel like I once did, please learn to set boundaries so that you don't have to learn the hard way. This journey has been brutal, and if Ihad to come back and do it all over again, I honestly don't know if I would. It's been that hard. Perhaps if I had been stronger from the very start, if I had learned my lessons faster, mylife might have taken a different turn.

But here's what I need you to know . . . Everything that

enters your life is there to teach and test you. So, can you handle it? Start by asking yourself: What will I no longer tolerate? Set your boundaries and create a plan. Don't be rigid—things will change—but having a plan will give you purpose. You need to become the best version of yourself. If I didn't have a feeling of purpose and something to wake up for, I wouldn't be here. My son was my purpose but also my dating app and Mind Jump Magazine gave me a reason to get upeach day.

One of my biggest weaknesses was my dyslexia. My reading and writing were so poor, and I used it as an excuse for far too long. But stagnation isn't growth. I realised that to grow, I had to learn. So, I asked myself: What are you hiding? What are your weaknesses?

What don't you love about yourself? Don't ignore it. Don't blame others. Do something about it. I felt stupid because I struggled to read and write, so I forced myself to improve. I hated it—it was like going to the dentist, a torturous ordeal filled with discomfort and pain. But I pushed myself out of my comfort zone, every single day.

For years, people struggled to understand my texts and emails, and I received more than my fair share of criticism. But I kept trying, and slowly, I got better. Then, I started writing articles—and people liked them. That small bit of encouragement boosted my confidence immensely. Over time, reading and writing transformed from painful tasks into activities I cherished. I no longer felt stupid; I began to feel intelligent, and that newfound confidence spurred me on to learn even more.

Here's the truth . . . Knowledge is power. I eventually ran small businesses and even found myself in leadership roles. Those experiences gave me a sense of authority and self-assurance. Another area I struggled with was my weight. I decided to do something about it—I got back into the gym and eliminated any excuses. Looking at myself today, I feel confident. I'm honest with myself and with others. I've made many mistakes, but I've learned from them, and I hope that by sharing my failures, I can help you avoid the same pitfalls.

So, tell me—what are you not being honest about? And more importantly, what are you going to do about it? Come on, you have one life. Don't waste these precious years. You are capable of so much more than you realise. I believe in you, and I want you to believe in yourself. Remember, there is only one of you in this world—and that's truly amazing, that's rare, and you are so lucky.

When we come into this world, we all have an assignment— a purpose. Maybe you're meant to be a mother, or a police officer, or even a prime minister. Whatever it is, you'll know, because if you're not happy, then you're not on your path. I believe that before we even entered this world, we chose our lessons, our challenges, and our struggles. And that means you are exactly where you're meant to be.

I know I've been on this planet many times—I feel it in every bone in my body. I know I've once lived a different life, with a personality different from the person I am now, and that journey was filled with pain and triumph. Even then, I had to open Pandora's box and face my inner demons. It made me feel sick inside, but in this life, I'm here to share those lessons.

Do I regret anything? No, I don't. What have I learned? That no one is coming to save you or love you in the way you think they will. Although we are never truly alone—we have God and our angels to guide and support us, if we ask for help. And that little voice in your gut? Listen to it. Don't bury your Pandora's box. I know it's hard, but facing it is how you grow. Every obstacle, every hardship, teaches us to become stronger, more resilient, and ultimately, more loving.

As I stand here today, I am not the same person I once was. I have learned how to overcome life's toughest challenges, and I am immensely grateful for the hardships. They have shaped me, taught me, and made me the best version of myself—a version that is kind, confident, and unyielding. I urge you to set your boundaries, to be honest about your weaknesses, and to take action. You have one life. Don't waste it. Embrace your journey, learn from your struggles, and write your next chapter with courage and conviction. I believe in you, and I want you to believe in yourself too.

If I Can Give You One Piece of Advice . . ., should you take anything away from reading this book . . . **trust your gut—it's your soul speaking to you**.

My self-worth used to be inextricably tied to material things, as though being surrounded by the latest gadgets or trendy clothes was the true measure of success. I remember desperately wanting those cool Adidas trainers, but we couldn't afford them. Instead, I had to settle for the Woolworths special—£2 black plimsolls. I was so embarrassed; I felt utterly worthless. That feeling stayed with me as I got older—if I didn't have the latest phone, perfect hair, or designer clothes, I felt inadequate. Looking back now, that mentality makes me cringe, to think that I once saw material wealth as something to achieve, as something to aspire to.

I've realised something truly fundamental. Some people who flaunt luxuries obtained them through questionable means—perhaps even by bending the law. And I had to ask myself: Why on earth had I been looking up to them? It's a bit like scrolling through Instagram and seeing so many flawless, beautiful images of people, portraying that they have it all. But when I met some of those people in real life, I didn't even recognise them. So, why was I allowing myself to be inspired by such superficiality? Why was I viewing material wealth as the pinnacle of success?

Honestly, I feel angry at myself for being so foolish back then. But now, I understand true wealth lies in good values and strong morals. Believe me, I've messed up many times—I've compromised my own values—but I've learned from it.

I used to worry obsessively about how my choices would impact my son, especially regarding the mental health implications of our situation. For years, I wondered whether staying with my ex until my son turned 18 would make things easier for him. But after countless conversations with child psychologists, therapists, and adults who had weathered similar storms, I realised something essential—a young child adapts easily.

A child's world is full of safety nets—family, friends, and school. My son never wanted to be in a toxic environment. Even as a child, he knew something was amiss. But once a child turns 18, their world expands, and the support systems crumble. That's when loneliness sets in, and the weight of everything becomes far heavier.

I've always been honest with my son and paid close attention to his feelings—ensuring we spent quality time together, whether reading, cuddling, or taking long walks. It's not about the quantity of time, but about being fully present. If you're a parent who only sees your child occasionally, remember that what truly matters is being there in the moment. Make every minute count. Be the present in their life.

So, here's the gist: if you're unhappy; if your relationships or your environment drain you—do something about it. We are only here for a short time, and each of us has a purpose.

Deep down, I believe we know what our purpose is. After all, we all agreed to this journeybefore we arrived on earth.

I used to believe that material things defined success. Now, I know that real success is measured by the love we share, the kindness we show, and the courage to live authentically. Ibelieve in you, and I want you to believe in yourself. Remember, there is only one of you in this world, and that in itself is amazing. So, check your priorities, set your boundaries, and above all, never lose sight of the fact that you are worthy of love—starting with the love yougive yourself.

Where is my tiara? It's back on my head where it belongs and I hope you find yours!

Thank you for reading.

Please check out Mind Jump Magazine—it's free. Set up an account with your name and email. And if you're ready to change your life, know that you have the power to write your next chapter. We hope you can join us—there's so much happening, from events and retreatsto networking opportunities and more.

Sending you so much love and light.

Little poems I wrote while in the dark.

The Wealth of Life

Wealth isn't money or fancy things, It's not about yachts or diamond rings. It's waking up healthy, feeling alright, It's laughing with family late into the night. It's time with friends, no rush, no race, Just being together in a cosy space. It's a helping hand, a smile passed on, A quick little chat when the day feels long. It's kids' silly jokes, a walk in the sun, Knowing you've done good when the day is done. It's not what you own, but what you give, That's the kind of wealth that helps you live. So here's to the wealth we can all afford—

Kindness, good health, and time we've stored. The richest of lives aren't built on gold, But on love and the moments we get to hold.

Life Is Like the Weather

Life is like the weather—you can't predict it You certainly can't control it

Some days, there's beautiful sunshine, and sometimes there's rain

The rain can be beautiful, especially when there's a rainbow, but at other times, it can cause chaos and disruption The storm clears the energy—but can also bring destruction and turmoil And then there's the snow—it looks absolutely beautiful and can be lots of fun—but it canalso bring challenges

Life is the weather

We change, we grow, and we need that change—although we may not always want the rainor storms, they help our crops grow and feed the earth

Appreciate each day, but be prepared for the rainy and stormy ones Just let life flow and grow Like the weather And remember—there is always sunshine after the rain.

By Lisa Holley PalmerLots of love, Lisa xx

Just want to add a thank you.

To the guys and girls who worked in the shop, when I cried, you gave me hope and a hug, when I had no money for food you helped. You are truly kind souls and I thank you from the bottom of my heart. You know who you are!